Excel 2007: Intermediate

Student Manual

Excel 2007: Intermediate

VP and GM, Training Group:	Michael Springer
Series Product Managers:	Charles G. Blum and Adam A. Wilcox
Writer:	Steve English
Developmental Editor:	Micky Markert
Copyeditor:	Catherine Oliver
Keytester:	Cliff Coryea
Series Designer:	Adam A. Wilcox
Cover Designer:	Abby Scholz

For more information contact:

Course Technology
25 Thomson Place
Boston, MA 02210

Or find us on the Web at: www.course.com

Trademarks

Disclaimers

1-4260-9778-6

Printed in the United States of America

1 2 3 4 5 WS 06 05 04 03

What is the Microsoft Business Certification Program?

The Microsoft Business Certification Program enables candidates to show that they have something exceptional to offer—proven expertise in Microsoft Office programs. The two certification tracks allow candidates to choose how they want to exhibit their skills, either through validating skills within a specific Microsoft product or taking their knowledge to the next level and combining Microsoft programs to show that they can apply multiple skill sets to complete more complex office tasks. Recognized by businesses and schools around the world, over 3 million certifications have been obtained in over 100 different countries. The Microsoft Business Certification Program is the only Microsoft-approved certification program of its kind.

What is the Microsoft Certified Application Specialist Certification?

Microsoft® CERTIFIED
Application Specialist

The Microsoft Certified Application Specialist Certification exams focus on validating specific skill sets within each of the Microsoft® Office system programs. The candidate can choose which exam(s) they want to take according to which skills they want to validate. The available Application Specialist exams include:

- Using Microsoft® Windows Vista™
- Using Microsoft® Office Word 2007
- Using Microsoft® Office Excel® 2007
- Using Microsoft® Office PowerPoint® 2007
- Using Microsoft® Office Access 2007
- Using Microsoft® Office Outlook® 2007

What is the Microsoft Certified Application Professional Certification?

Microsoft® CERTIFIED
Application Professional

The Microsoft Certified Application Professional Certification exams focus on a candidate's ability to use the 2007 Microsoft® Office system to accomplish industry-agnostic functions, for example Budget Analysis and Forecasting, or Content Management and Collaboration. The available Application Professional exams currently include:

- Organizational Support
- Creating and Managing Presentations
- Content Management and Collaboration
- Budget Analysis and Forecasting

What do the Microsoft Business Certification Vendor of Approved Courseware logos represent?

Microsoft CERTIFIED Application Specialist | Approved Courseware

Microsoft CERTIFIED Application Professional | Approved Courseware

The logos validate that the courseware has been approved by the Microsoft® Business Certification Vendor program and that these courses cover objectives that will be included in the relevant exam. It also means that after utilizing this courseware, you may be prepared to pass the exams required to become a Microsoft Certified Application Specialist or Microsoft Certified Application Professional.

For more information

To learn more about the Microsoft Certified Application Specialist or Professional exams[1], visit www.microsoft.com/learning/msbc.

To learn about other Microsoft Certified Application Specialist approved courseware from Course Technology, visit www.courseilt.com.

[1]The availability of Microsoft Certified Application exams varies by Microsoft Office program, program version, and language. Visit www.microsoft.com/learning for exam availability.

Contents

Introduction

After reading this introduction, you will know how to:

A Use Course Technology ILT manuals in general.

B Use prerequisites, a target student description, course objectives, and a skills inventory to properly set your expectations for the course.

C Re-key this course after class.

Topic A: About the manual

Course Technology ILT philosophy

Course Technology ILT manuals facilitate your learning by providing structured interaction with the software itself. While we provide text to explain difficult concepts, the hands-on activities are the focus of our courses. By paying close attention as your instructor leads you through these activities, you will learn the skills and concepts effectively.

We believe strongly in the instructor-led class. During class, focus on your instructor. Our manuals are designed and written to facilitate your interaction with your instructor, and not to call attention to manuals themselves.

We believe in the basic approach of setting expectations, delivering instruction, and providing summary and review afterwards. For this reason, lessons begin with objectives and end with summaries. We also provide overall course objectives and a course summary to provide both an introduction to and closure on the entire course.

Manual components

The manuals contain these major components:

- Table of contents
- Introduction
- Units
- Course summary
- Quick reference
- Glossary
- Index

Each element is described below.

Table of contents

The table of contents acts as a learning roadmap.

Introduction

The introduction contains information about our training philosophy and our manual components, features, and conventions. It contains target student, prerequisite, objective, and setup information for the specific course.

Units

Units are the largest structural component of the course content. A unit begins with a title page that lists objectives for each major subdivision, or topic, within the unit. Within each topic, conceptual and explanatory information alternates with hands-on activities. Units conclude with a summary comprising one paragraph for each topic, and an independent practice activity that gives you an opportunity to practice the skills you've learned.

The conceptual information takes the form of text paragraphs, exhibits, lists, and tables. The activities are structured in two columns, one telling you what to do, the other providing explanations, descriptions, and graphics.

Course summary

This section provides a text summary of the entire course. It is useful for providing closure at the end of the course. The course summary also indicates the next course in this series, if there is one, and lists additional resources you might find useful as you continue to learn about the software.

Quick reference

The quick reference is an at-a-glance job aid summarizing some of the more common features of the software.

Index

The index at the end of this manual makes it easy for you to find information about a particular software component, feature, or concept.

Manual conventions

We've tried to keep the number of elements and the types of formatting to a minimum in the manuals. This aids in clarity and makes the manuals more classically elegant looking. But there are some conventions and icons you should know about.

Item	Description
Italic text	In conceptual text, indicates a new term or feature.
Bold text	In unit summaries, indicates a key term or concept. In an independent practice activity, indicates an explicit item that you select, choose, or type.
`Code font`	Indicates code or syntax.

`Longer strings of ►`
`code will look ►`
`like this.`
	In the hands-on activities, any code that's too long to fit on a single line is divided into segments by one or more continuation characters (►). This code should be entered as a continuous string of text.

Select **bold item**	In the left column of hands-on activities, bold sans-serif text indicates an explicit item that you select, choose, or type.
Keycaps like ↵ ENTER	Indicate a key on the keyboard you must press.

Hands-on activities

The hands-on activities are the most important parts of our manuals. They are divided into two primary columns. The "Here's how" column gives short instructions to you about what to do. The "Here's why" column provides explanations, graphics, and clarifications. Here's a sample:

Do it!

A-1: Creating a commission formula

Here's how	Here's why
1 Open Sales	This is an oversimplified sales compensation worksheet. It shows sales totals, commissions, and incentives for five sales reps.
2 Observe the contents of cell F4	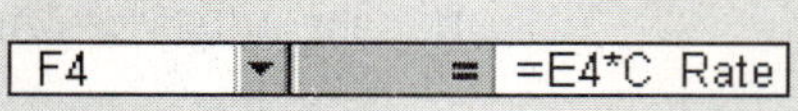 The commission rate formulas use the name "C_Rate" instead of a value for the commission rate.

For these activities, we have provided a collection of data files designed to help you learn each skill in a real-world business context. As you work through the activities, you will modify and update these files. Of course, you might make a mistake and therefore want to re-key the activity starting from scratch. To make it easy to start over, you will rename each data file at the end of the first activity in which the file is modified. Our convention for renaming files is to add the word "My" to the beginning of the file name. In the above activity, for example, a file called "Sales" is being used for the first time. At the end of this activity, you would save the file as "My sales," thus leaving the "Sales" file unchanged. If you make a mistake, you can start over using the original "Sales" file.

In some activities, however, it might not be practical to rename the data file. If you want to retry one of these activities, ask your instructor for a fresh copy of the original data file.

Topic B: Setting your expectations

Properly setting your expectations is essential to your success. This topic will help you do that by providing:

- Prerequisites for this course
- A description of the target student
- A list of the objectives for the course
- A skills assessment for the course

Course prerequisites

Before taking this course, you should be familiar with personal computers and the use of a keyboard and a mouse. Furthermore, this course assumes that you've completed the *Excel 2007: Basic* course or have equivalent experience.

Target student

Before taking this course, you should be comfortable using a personal computer and Microsoft Windows XP. You should have some experience using Microsoft Excel. You will get the most out of this course if your goal is to become proficient in such tasks as consolidating data, using advanced chart formatting options, sorting and filtering lists, using special formatting options, using templates, using error tracing features, protecting worksheets, and linking worksheets and workbooks.

Microsoft Certified Application Specialist certification

This course is designed to help you pass the Microsoft Certified Application Specialist exam for Excel 2007. For comprehensive certification training, you should complete all of the following courses:

- *Excel 2007: Basic*
- *Excel 2007: Intermediate*
- *Excel 2007: Advanced*

Course objectives

These overall course objectives will give you an idea about what to expect from the course. It is also possible that they will help you see that this course is not the right one for you. If you think you either lack the prerequisite knowledge or already know most of the subject matter to be covered, you should let your instructor know that you think you are misplaced in the class.

Note: In addition to the general objectives listed below, specific Microsoft Certified Application Specialist exam objectives are listed at the beginning of each topic (where applicable). To download a complete mapping of exam objectives to ILT Series content, go to: www.virtualrom.com/658ACD612

After completing this course, you will know how to:

- Link worksheets by using 3-D formulas; add a Watch window; create and manage links between workbooks; and create a workspace.
- Apply special and custom number formats; control the display of zero values; use functions to format text; create, apply, and modify styles; apply and modify themes; merge and split cells; change the orientation of data in cells; transpose data; and add background color and a watermark.
- Create an outline and consolidate data; create subtotals in a list; and use multiple subtotal functions.
- Define and apply cell and range names; use names in formulas; and define and apply 3-D names.
- Sort lists by columns; filter lists based on complex criteria and copy filtered results to another range; create and format a table and add rows and columns; apply structured referencing; name tables; and create functions with [#This row].
- Save and publish a worksheet as a Web page; insert and edit hyperlinks; publish a worksheet as a PDF file, and send a worksheet as an e-mail attachment.
- Format data points; create combination charts and trendlines; and add and format graphic elements.
- Use auditing features; add comments to cells and workbooks; protect a worksheet or part of a worksheet; share, merge, and track changes in a workbook; find and remove hidden and personal data from a workbook; and mark a workbook as final.
- Change Excel's default application settings; work with Excel templates; and create and manage templates.

Skills inventory

Use the following form to gauge your skill level entering the class. For each skill listed, rate your familiarity from 1 to 5, with five being the most familiar. *This is not a test.* Rather, it is intended to provide you with an idea of where you're starting from at the beginning of class. If you're wholly unfamiliar with all the skills, you might not be ready for the class. If you think you already understand all of the skills, you might need to move on to the next course in the series. In either case, you should let your instructor know as soon as possible.

Skill	1	2	3	4	5
Switching between workbooks, and copying a worksheet to another workbook					
Creating 3-D formulas to link worksheets and workbooks					
Adding a Watch window					
Linking workbooks, creating external links, and redirecting links					
Creating a workspace					
Applying built-in and custom number formats					
Using functions to format text					
Creating, modifying, and applying styles					
Applying and modifying themes					
Merging and splitting cells, and changing cell orientation					
Transposing data					
Adding backgrounds and watermarks					
Creating outlines to summarize and consolidate data					
Creating subtotals and using multiple subtotal functions					
Naming cells and ranges, and using names in formulas					
Modifying and deleting names					
Defining and applying 3-D names					
Sorting and filtering lists					
Using advanced filtering options					
Creating, formatting, and modifying tables					
Applying structured referencing in table formulas					
Calculating sum, average, and count values in a filtered table list					

Skill	**1**	**2**	**3**	**4**	**5**
Saving and publishing a worksheet as a Web page					
Saving a workbook as a PDF file					
Inserting and editing hyperlinks					
Sending worksheets via e-mail					
Using advanced chart formatting options					
Creating combination charts and trendlines					
Inserting and formatting graphic elements in charts					
Using auditing features					
Adding comments to worksheets and workbooks					
Protecting a worksheet					
Sharing, merging, and tracking changes in workbooks					
Using the Document Inspector and marking workbooks as final					
Changing default application settings					
Using built-in templates, and creating and managing templates					

Topic C: Re-keying the course

If you have the proper hardware and software, you can re-key this course after class. This section explains what you'll need in order to do so, and how to do it.

Hardware requirements

Your personal computer should have:

- A keyboard and a mouse
- Pentium 500 MHz processor (or higher)
- At least 256 MB RAM
- 2 GB of available hard drive space
- CD-ROM drive
- SVGA at 1024×768, or higher resolution monitor

Software requirements

You will need the following software:

- Windows XP, Windows Vista, or Windows Server 2003
- Microsoft Office 2007
- The Microsoft Save as PDF or XPS Add-in for 2007 Microsoft Office programs. (If this is not installed, you will not be able to complete Activity C-1 in the unit titled "Web and Internet features.")
- Adobe Reader 8 or later, for viewing PDF files in Activity C-1 in the unit titled "Web and Internet features."

Network requirements

The following network components and connectivity are also required for this course:

- Internet access, for the following purposes:
  - Updating the Windows operating system and Microsoft Office 2007 at update.microsoft.com
  - Downloading the Student Data files (if necessary).
  - Downloading the Microsoft Save as PDF or XPS Add-in for 2007 Microsoft Office programs from www.microsoft.com/downloads. (If this add-in is not available, you will not be able to complete Activity C-1 in the unit titled "Web and Internet features.")
  - Downloading Adobe Reader 8 from www.adobe.com. (If this is not installed, you will not be able to view the PDF file created in Activity C-1 in the unit titled "Web and Internet features.")
  - Downloading document templates from Microsoft Office Online. (If online templates are not available, you will not be able to complete Activity B-1 in the unit titled "Templates and settings.")

Setup instructions to re-key the course

Before you re-key the course, you will need to perform the following steps.

1 Download the latest critical updates and service packs from www.windowsupdate.com.

2 From the Control Panel, open the Display Properties dialog box and apply the following settings:

- Theme — Windows XP
- Screen resolution — 1024 by 768 pixels
- Color quality — High (24 bit) or higher

If you choose not to apply these display settings, your screens might not match the screen shots in this manual.

3 If you are using the same computer used in class, reset any Excel 2007 defaults that you have changed. If you do not wish to reset the defaults, you can still re-key the course, but some activities might not work exactly as documented.

a Click the Office Button and click Excel Options to open the Excel Options dialog box.

b On the Popular page, under "Top options for working with Excel," click Edit Custom Lists. Delete the custom list containing North, South, East, Central, and West. Click OK to close the Custom Lists dialog box.

c Under "Personalize your copy of Microsoft Office," remove the name from the User name box and replace it with a more generic name, such as Student01 or User01.

d On the Save page, under Save Workbooks, confirm that the default file location is C:\Documents and Settings*User_name*\My Documents.

e On the Advanced page, under Display, verify that under "For cells with comments, show," the "Indicators only, and comments on hover" option is selected.

f On the Advanced page, under "Display options for this worksheet," check "Show a zero in cells that have zero value."

g On the Customize page, remove any commands added to the Quick Access toolbar. The only commands that should be left on it are Save, Undo, and Redo.

h Click OK to save these settings and close the Excel Options dialog box.

4 Remove the Sample test and My OS invoice templates from the Templates folder. To do so, navigate to C:\Documents and Settings*User_name*\Application Data\Microsoft\Templates, and delete the templates.

5 Create a folder named Student Data at the root of the hard drive. For a standard hard drive setup, this will be C:\Student Data.

6 Download the Student Data files for the course. (If you do not have an Internet connection, you can ask your instructor for a copy of the data files on a disk.)

a Connect to www.courseilt.com/ilt_downloads.cfm.

b Click the link for Microsoft Excel 2007 to display a page of course listings, and then click the link for Excel 2007: Intermediate.

c Click the link for downloading the Student Data files, and follow the instructions that appear on your screen.

7 Copy the data files to the Student Data folder.

CertBlaster exam preparation software

If you plan to take the Microsoft Certified Application Specialist exam for Excel 2007, we encourage you to use the CertBlaster pre- and post-assessment software that comes with this course. To download and install your free software:

1. Go to www.courseilt.com/certblaster.
2. Click the link for Excel 2007.
3. Save the .EXE file to a folder on your hard drive. (Note: If you skip this step, the CertBlaster software will not install correctly.)
4. Click Start and choose Run.
5. Click Browse and then navigate to the folder that contains the .EXE file.
6. Select the .EXE file and click Open.
7. Click OK and follow the on-screen instructions. When prompted for the password, enter **c_602**.

Unit 1

Using multiple worksheets and workbooks

Unit time: 60 minutes

Complete this unit, and you'll know how to:

A Switch between workbooks, and copy a sheet from one workbook to another

B Create 3-D formulas to link worksheets, and add a Watch window.

C Create and manage linked workbooks.

D Create a workspace to manage workbooks.

Control- Pg up / Pg down

Topic A: Using multiple workbooks

This topic covers the following Microsoft Certified Application Specialist exam objective for Excel 2007.

#	Objective
1.5.1	**Copy worksheets** • Between workbooks

Opening and switching between multiple workbooks

Explanation

For various reasons, you may want to have more than one workbook open at a time. You can open and work with as many workbooks as your computer memory permits. Each workbook has its own window and a unique button on the Windows taskbar.

To switch between workbooks, you can click each workbook's taskbar button. You can also activate the View tab, and in the Window group, click Switch Windows, as shown in Exhibit 1-1.

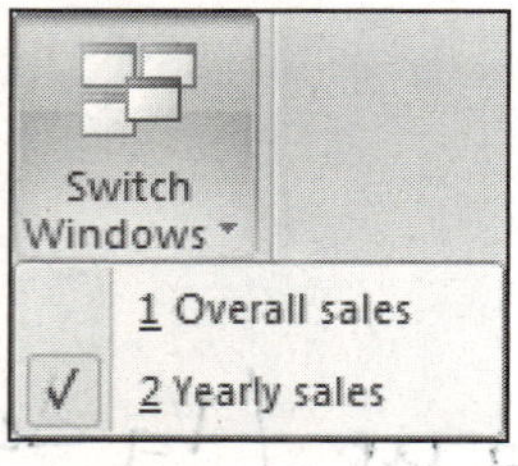

Exhibit 1-1: The Switch Windows menu on the View tab

Do it!

A-1: Switching between workbooks

Here's how	Here's why
1 Open Microsoft Excel 2007	Choose Start, All Programs, Microsoft Office, Microsoft Office Excel 2007.
Close the blank workbook	
2 Open Yearly sales	In the current unit folder.
Open Overall sales	

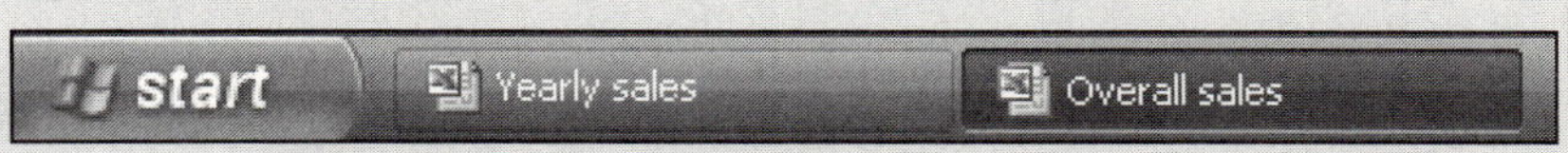

Here's how	Here's why
	A separate button for each workbook appears in the Windows taskbar. (Your taskbar might look different depending on the files that are open and the items in the Quick Launch toolbar.)
3 Click the **Yearly sales** taskbar button	To activate the Yearly sales workbook.
4 Activate the View tab	
In the Window group, click **Switch Windows**	To see the list of open workbooks, as shown in Exhibit 1-1. The names of the two open workbooks appear, with a check mark beside the active workbook.
5 Click **Overall sales**	To switch to that workbook.
6 Close the workbook	If prompted, don't save changes.
Switch to Yearly sales and save it as **My yearly sales**	

Copying worksheets between workbooks

Explanation

You can copy worksheets between workbooks as easily as copying worksheets within a workbook. Be aware, however, that worksheets containing formulas or charts based on data elsewhere in that workbook might become inaccurate when moved to a new workbook.

To copy a worksheet to another workbook, make sure the target workbook is open. Then, do the following:

1. Activate the worksheet you want to copy.
2. On the Home tab, in the Cells group, click Format to display the Format menu.
3. Under Organize Sheets, choose Move or Copy Sheet to open the Move or Copy dialog box.
4. In the To book list, select the name of the workbook you want to copy to.
5. In the Before sheet list, select the name of the sheet before which you want to place the copy, or choose (move to end).
6. Check Create a Copy.
7. Click OK.

You can also open the Move or Copy dialog box by right-clicking the worksheet and choosing Move or Copy.

Do it!

A-2: Copying a worksheet to another workbook

Here's how	Here's why
1 Open Product	In the current unit folder. You'll copy the worksheet Product details to another workbook.
2 Activate the Home tab	
In the Cells group, click **Format**	To display the Format menu.
Choose **Move or Copy Sheet…**	To open the Move or Copy dialog box.
3 From the To book list, select **My yearly sales**	This is the workbook to which you'll copy the worksheet.
4 In the Before sheet list, select **(move to end)**	To position the copy as the last sheet in the My yearly sales workbook.
5 Check **Create a copy**	
6 Click **OK**	To create the copy and place it in the new workbook. The My yearly sales workbook becomes active, showing the copy of the Product details worksheet.
7 Switch to Product	
Close the workbook	If prompted, don't save changes.
8 Update My yearly sales	

Topic B: Linking worksheets with 3-D formulas

This topic covers the following Microsoft Certified Application Specialist exam objective for Excel 2007.

#	Objective
3.1.2	**Create formulas that reference data from other worksheets or workbooks** • Using sales figures from other worksheets, create summary sheets that have four titles for four fiscal quarters' total sales figures

Syntax of 3-D formulas

Explanation

A *3-D formula* refers to the same cell or range in multiple worksheets. For example, the formula =SUM(North:West!B5) sums the data in the B5 cells in the range North:West in four worksheets. The syntax for referring to cells in another worksheet is:

```
worksheet_name!reference
```

Here, `worksheet_name` refers to the name of the worksheet that provides the data, `reference` is the name of the cell or range, and ! is the divider between the worksheet reference and the cell reference.

Inserting a 3-D reference

To insert a 3-D reference into a formula:

1. Enter the formula until the point where you need a value from another worksheet to complete the formula.
2. Activate the first worksheet you want to refer to.
3. While pressing Shift, activate the last worksheet you want to refer to in the formula.
4. Select the cell or range containing the values you want the formula to refer to.
5. Complete the formula and press Enter. Exhibit 1-2 shows a worksheet with 3-D formulas applied (the results of Activity A-1).

Product	Qtr1	Qtr2	Qtr3	Qtr4
Anise Seeds	$2,725	$2,114	$2,467	$2,676
Asafoetida Powder	$2,674	$2,535	$2,553	$3,208
Basil Leaf (Whole)	$29,783	$28,751	$23,478	$33,117
Bay Leaf (Whole)	$1,773	$2,780	$2,620	$2,607
Caraway Seed (Whole)	$2,263	$3,084	$2,368	$2,112
Cardamom Seed (Whole)	$1,277	$2,199	$1,618	$2,619
Cardamom Seed (Ground)	$2,489	$2,760	$2,561	$2,804
Catnip Leaf	$3,447	$1,466	$1,870	$2,950
Celery Seed (Whole)	$24,232	$28,437	$23,697	$18,124
Chamomile Flowers	$1,770	$2,591	$2,323	$2,209

Exhibit 1-2: A worksheet with 3-D formulas applied in Activity B-1

Do it!

B-1: Creating 3-D formulas

Here's how	Here's why
1 In the My yearly sales workbook, activate the North sheet	
2 Activate the South, East, and West sheets	Click each tab. Each worksheet contains quarterly sales for a different sales region.
Activate the Creating 3-D formula worksheet	
3 In B5, type **=SUM(**	To begin the function.
4 Activate the North worksheet	To select the first worksheet in the 3-D reference.
Press SHIFT and activate the West worksheet	To specify the worksheet range North:West in the function. The color of the four worksheet tabs in the range changes to white.
Release SHIFT	
5 In the active worksheet, select B5	To select the cell containing the first-quarter anise seed sales in each of the four selected worksheets.
Type **)** and press ↵ ENTER	To complete the 3-D formula. The Creating 3-D formula worksheet automatically becomes the active worksheet again.
6 Select B5	In the Creating 3-D formula worksheet.
Observe the formula bar	 In the formula, North:West refers to the worksheet range North through West (North, South, East, and West), ! is the divider between the worksheet and cell references, and B5 is the cell address.
7 Copy the formula in B5 to the rest of the range B5:E14	(Use the fill handle in the bottom-right corner of B5.) To calculate the total quarterly sales for each product.
8 Deselect the cells	Click anywhere in the worksheet.
9 Observe the worksheet	The worksheet should resemble Exhibit 1-2.
10 Update the workbook	

Adding a Watch window

Explanation

Excel formulas can refer to cells or ranges in other worksheets, or a range of worksheets, within a workbook. This type of formula creates a link between worksheets. When two worksheets are linked, any change that you make in the source cell is automatically updated in the linked cell. You can observe this effect by adding a *Watch window* to the source cell. This way, you don't need to navigate to the other worksheets to see the updated information.

To add a Watch window:

1. Select the cell to which you want to add a Watch window.
2. Activate the Formulas tab.
3. In the Formula Auditing group, click Watch Window.
4. Click Add Watch to open the Watch Window dialog box.
5. Click Add to place this cell in the Watch window.

Do it!

B-2: Adding a Watch window

Here's how	Here's why
1 Activate the Report worksheet	This worksheet contains summarized data from the North, South, East, and West worksheets. You'll add a Watch window.
Select B5	 B5 has the value $2,725, which is the sum of all cells with the address B5 in the worksheet range North:West. In other words, it is the bonus first-quarter sales of anise seeds from all four regions.
2 Activate the Formulas tab	On the Ribbon.
3 In the Formula Auditing group, click **Watch Window**	To open a Watch window.
Click **Add Watch**	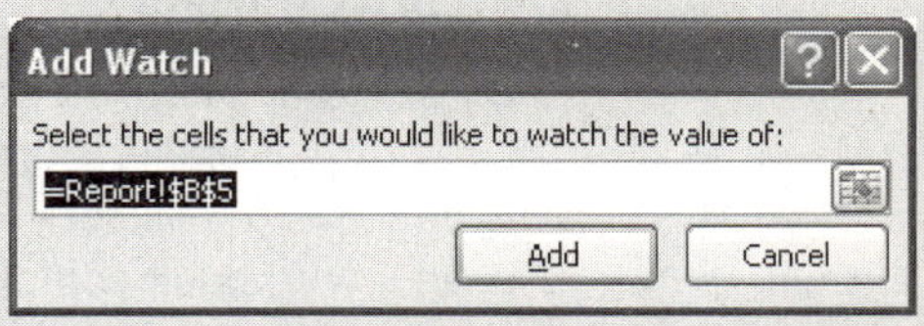 To open the Add Watch dialog box. Cell B5 in the Report worksheet is automatically selected because that is the active cell.
Click **Add**	To select this cell and add it to the Watch window. The workbook, sheet, cell, value, and formula for B5 appear in the Watch window.
4 Activate the North worksheet	The Watch window remains visible, no matter which worksheet is active. You'll change the value of B5 in this worksheet and observe the change in the linked cell in the Watch window.
In B5, enter **1000**	In the Watch window, the value in B5 of the Report worksheet is updated to $3,191.
5 Close the Watch window	
6 Update and close the workbook	

Topic C: Linking workbooks

Explanation

Just as you can link multiple worksheets within a workbook, you can also link multiple workbooks. You can do this by writing a formula in one workbook that refers to a cell, range, or name in another workbook. References to other workbooks are called *external references*. You can maintain workbook links even if the workbook that is referred to is renamed.

External links

The syntax for referring to cells in another workbook is:

```
'[workbook_name]worksheet_name'!reference
```

Here, `workbook_name` refers to the name of the workbook that provides the data, and `worksheet_name` refers to the name of the worksheet in the source workbook. At the end of the formula, `reference` is the name of the cell or range, and `!` is the divider between the worksheet reference and the cell reference.

Security warnings

By default, Microsoft Excel 2007 is configured to prompt you when a workbook that has external links requires those links to be updated. This is a security consideration that is intended to protect your workbooks from viruses and other malicious code. When you open a workbook containing external links that need updating, Excel displays a security warning, shown in Exhibit 1-3, below the Ribbon.

Exhibit 1-3: The security warning appears between the Ribbon and the formula bar

To enable the updating of links between workbooks:

1. In the security warning, click Options to open the Microsoft Office Security Options dialog box, shown in Exhibit 1-4.
2. Select "Enable this content."
3. Click OK.

Exhibit 1-4: The Microsoft Office Security Options dialog box

Do it!

C-1: Examining external links in a worksheet

Here's how	Here's why
1 Open Overall Sales	
Save the workbook as **My overall sales**	
2 In the security warning, click **Options**	(The security warning appears between the Ribbon and the formula bar.) The Microsoft Office Security Options dialog box appears.
Select **Enable this content**	To enable automatic updating of the workbook links.
Click **OK**	To close the dialog box. The security warning disappears.
3 Activate the Quarterly revenue worksheet	(If necessary.) This worksheet contains the quarterly revenue report for four sales regions. The My overall sales workbook is linked to the Yearly sales workbook. Column C of the Quarterly revenue worksheet contains total sales for the first quarter.
Select C6	
Observe the formula bar	fx ='[Yearly sales.xlsx]North'!$B$15 The formula bar displays the path and source of the link. (Your path might look different depending on how folders are configured on your PC.) In the formula bar, Yearly sales is the source workbook, North is the worksheet, and $B$15 is the cell address to which the formula is linked. The current value in this cell is 14,074.
4 Open the Yearly sales workbook	The North worksheet is active.
Edit B5 to read **1000**	The value in B15 changes from $14,074 to $14,540.
5 Activate the My overall sales workbook	To view the changes in the linked workbook. In the Quarterly revenue worksheet, the value in C6 has also changed from 14,074 to 14,540.
6 Update the workbook	

Creating external links

Explanation

When you build formulas that refer to worksheets in other workbooks, the workbook that contains the formula is called the *destination workbook*, and the workbook to which the formula refers is called the *source workbook*.

To create an external link:

1. Open the destination workbook.
2. Select the cell where you want to enter the formula.
3. Type the equals sign (=).
4. Activate the source workbook.
5. Select the cell that you want the formula to refer to.
6. Press Enter.

Region	Total expenses	Total sales	Profit/Loss
North	$13,395	$62,216	$48,821
South	$89,000	$88,358	($642)
East	$21,947	$76,345	$54,398
West	$15,530	$60,678	$45,148

Exhibit 1-5: A worksheet with external references after Activity B-3

Do it!

C-2: Creating external links in a worksheet

Here's how	Here's why
1 Activate the Total revenue worksheet	You'll create a new link between the My overall sales workbook and the Yearly sales workbook. The Profit/Loss column displays profit or loss data for each region. Currently, the Total sales column does not contain any data.
2 In C5, enter **=**	
Activate the Yearly sales workbook	The North worksheet is active.
Select F15	fx ='[Yearly sales.xlsx]North'!$F$15
	To enter a linked reference. Yearly sales is the workbook name, North is the worksheet name, and $F$15 is the cell reference.
Press ENTER	To enter the external reference. The My overall sales workbook becomes active. C5 shows the formula's result, which is $62,216.
3 Enter the external references for the remaining regions	(Remember to enter these as linked references.) Type the =, activate the respective region tabs of the Yearly sales workbook, select the total sales value in F15, and press Enter. The worksheet will resemble Exhibit 1-5.
4 Update the workbook	

Maintaining workbook links

Explanation

You can change the name of a workbook even if it is linked to another workbook. If both the source and destination workbooks are open, the link gets updated automatically. If you don't have the destination workbook open, you can still redirect the links by using the Connections group on the Data tab.

To redirect links:

1 Activate the Data tab.
2 In the Connections group, click Edit Links to open the Edit Links dialog box, shown in Exhibit 1-6.
3 From the Source file list, select the source workbook whose links you want to redirect.
4 Click the Change Source button to open the Change Source dialog box.
5 Select the name of the workbook to which you want to redirect the link. Click OK to return to the Edit Links dialog box.
6 Click Close to close the Edit Links dialog box.

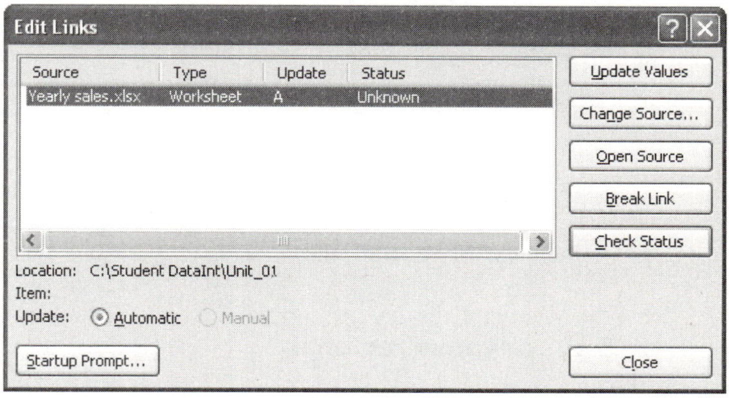

Exhibit 1-6: The Edit Links dialog box

Do it!

C-3: Editing links

Here's how	Here's why
1 Select C5	fx ='[Yearly sales.xlsx]North'!$F$15 (In the Total revenue worksheet of the My overall sales workbook.) The formula in the formula bar contains a reference to the Yearly sales workbook.
2 Activate the Yearly sales workbook	
Save the workbook as **My regional sales**	Saving the source file with a different name will automatically update the link in the destination file.
3 Activate the My overall sales workbook	
Select C5	fx ='[My regional sales.xlsx]North'!$F$15 (If necessary.) To view the updated link. The formula now contains a reference to My regional sales instead of to Yearly sales.
4 Update and close My overall sales	
5 Save the My regional sales workbook as **My new regional sales**	
6 Open My overall sales	The security warning appears. (If it does not appear, skip the next part of this step.)
Enable the content	(In the security warning, click Options. In the dialog box, select Enable this content and click OK.) To allow the automatic updating of external links.
7 Select C5	(If necessary.) The formula still refers to My regional sales.xlsx.
8 Activate the Data tab	You'll edit the links to refer to another workbook.
In the Connections group, click **Edit Links**	To open the Edit Links dialog box. The name of the source workbook is shown as My regional sales.xlsx.
Click **Change Source**	To open the Change Source: My regional sales.xlsx dialog box.
In the list of files, double-click **My new regional sales**	In the source list, the name of the workbook is now My new regional sales.xlsx.

9	Click **Close**	
	Observe the formula bar	The reference to My regional sales.xlsx has changed to My new regional sales.xlsx.
10	Update the workbook	

Topic D: Managing workbooks

This topic covers the following Microsoft Certified Application Specialist exam objective for Excel 2007.

#	Objective
1.4.3	Open and arrange new windows

Viewing multiple workbooks

Explanation

If you find that you repeatedly use the same set of workbooks, you can save them as a workspace. A *workspace* is a logical container of related workbooks that retains page setups, window sizes, and display settings. A workspace does not save the workbooks themselves, so you'll still need to save changes in each workbook individually.

Workspaces

While working with multiple workbooks, you can arrange them in a specific way on the screen to maximize the data you can see. Excel calls this arrangement a workspace. You can save this arrangement in a workspace file, which stores the position and size of the window for each open workbook. By default, Excel saves the workspace file with the name "resume." You can rename the file if you use different workspace files for different workbooks.

To create a workspace:

1. Open all the workbooks that you want to save together as a workspace.
2. Set the window sizes, screen magnifications, and any other display settings as you want them to be whenever you open the workspace.
3. Activate the View tab.
4. In the Window group, click Save Workspace to open the Save Workspace dialog box.
5. Specify a name and location for the workspace, and then click Save.

To open a workspace, select it from the Open dialog box.

Do it!

D-1: Creating a workspace

Here's how	Here's why
1 Activate the View tab	You'll arrange the two open workbooks and save the resulting workspace.
2 In the Window group, click **Arrange All**	To open the Arrange Windows dialog box.
Select **Vertical**	
Click **OK**	The open workbooks are both displayed, with a vertical divider between them.
3 Activate the My overall sales workbook	(If necessary.) Click anywhere on the worksheet.
Change the magnification to **75%**	Click the Zoom button on the taskbar and select 75% from the Zoom dialog box, or drag the slider until the Zoom button reads 75%.
4 Change the magnification for My new regional sales to **75%**	
5 In the Window group, click **Save Workspace**	To open the Save Workspace dialog box. By default, Workspaces is selected in the Save as type list.
Navigate to the current unit folder	If necessary.
Observe the default name in the File name box	The default file name is "resume."
Edit the File name box to read **My sales**	
6 Click **Save**	To save the workspace. If a message box appears asking if you want to save workbook changes, click Yes.
7 Close all open workbooks	
8 Display the Open dialog box	
Select **My sales**	
Click **Open**	The My new regional sales and My overall sales workbooks appear just as they did when you saved the workspace.
9 Open My yearly sales	You'll add another workbook to the workspace.

10	Open the Arrange Windows dialog box	In the Window group, click Arrange All.
	Select **Tiled**	
	Click **OK**	To close the dialog box and tile the open windows.
11	Open the Save Workspace dialog box	(Activate the View tab. In the Window group, click Save Workspace.) In the File name box, My sales is selected.
	Click **Save**	A message box asks if you want to replace the existing workspace.
	Click **Yes**	If a message box asks if you want to save workbook changes, click Yes.
12	Close all open workbooks	
13	Open My sales	The three workbooks appear as they did when you saved the workspace.
14	Close all open workbooks	If you're prompted to save changes, click No.

Unit summary: Using multiple worksheets and workbooks

Topic A In this topic, you learned how to switch between open workbooks and how to copy a worksheet from one workbook to another.

Topic B In this topic, you learned how to create **3-D formulas** to perform calculations across multiple worksheets. You also learned that Excel automatically updates the data in **destination** cells if you change the data in the **source** cells. You observed this in the **Watch window** without navigating between worksheets.

Topic C In this topic, you learned how to create **external links** to data in another workbook. You learned that data is automatically updated in the destination workbook when you change the data in the source workbook. You also learned how to use the **Edit Links dialog box** to change links in destination workbooks.

Topic D In this topic, you saved the display settings of several workbooks as a **workspace**, making it easier to open and work on them simultaneously.

Independent practice activity

In this activity, you will create 3-D formulas, and create and update external links. You'll open multiple workbooks at the same time, arrange them in a workspace, and save the workspace.

1. Open Practice sales (from the current unit folder), and save it as **My practice sales**. Open Product (from the current unit folder), and save it as **My product**. (You might need to maximize the windows.)
2. Activate the Report worksheet of the My practice sales workbook.
3. Create 3-D formulas to calculate the total sales (in $) for all products in all four regions. The formula for calculating total sales is **Qty Sold * Price**. Qty Sold for each region is stored in the respective region worksheets of the My Practice sales workbook. Prices are stored in the My product workbook.

   To do this for the North region, in My practice sales, activate Report and type = in B5. In My product, select C5. In the formula bar, make the reference to C5 relative by removing the $ signs before C and 5. Then, type * after C5 in the formula bar. Click the **North** tab in My practice sales, select B5, and press Enter. Use AutoFill to obtain the values for the rest of the Products under North.

   Using the same technique, create formulas for C5:E5, and use AutoFill to obtain the values for the remaining regions and products. When you're done, compare your results with Exhibit 1-7.
4. Update and close My practice sales. Close the My Product workbook.
5. Open the Yearly sales workbook. Open Overall sales and save it as **My practice overall sales**. Activate the Quarterly revenue worksheet of the My practice overall sales workbook. Verify that the Quarterly revenue worksheet is linked to the Yearly sales workbook.
6. Change the name of the Yearly sales workbook to **My annual sales**. (Save the workbook under the new name.)
7. Verify that the source of the link is updated in the My practice overall sales workbook.

8 Arrange the open workbooks horizontally in the Excel window.

9 Create a workspace named **My practice sales** that saves the current display settings.

10 Update and close both workbooks.

	A	B	C	D	E
1		**Outlander Spices**			
2		**Bonus sales for all regions**			
3					
4	**Product**	**North**	**South**	**East**	**West**
5	Cassia	$5,372,210	$2,773,022	$2,646,600	$5,025,112
6	Catnip Leaf	$5,861,990	$1,218,444	$3,025,701	$2,747,250
7	Celery Seed (Whole)	$383,650	$677,865	$328,505	$909,246
8	Celery Seed (Ground)	$4,198,897	$2,614,144	$4,363,487	$3,265,665
9	Chamomile Flowers	$69,156	$286,677	$492,055	$253,669
10	Chili Pepper Powder	$2,266,212	$5,544,111	$4,082,834	$2,125,811
11	Chinese Star Anise (Ground)	$1,922,761	$4,358,487	$2,488,171	$473,145
12	Chinese Star Anise (Whole)	$697,750	$7,128,062	$931,406	$4,509,601
13	Chives	$7,725,468	$4,092,269	$2,398,023	$448,908
14	Cilantro Flakes	$7,938,853	$2,884,557	$1,442,793	$1,953,937

Exhibit 1-7: A sample of the My practice sales workbook after Step 3

Review questions

1 What is a 3-D formula?

2 What is the advantage of a Watch window?

3 How do you redirect a workbook link?

4 What is a workspace?

5 When you save a workspace, are the workbooks themselves also saved individually?

Unit 2

Advanced formatting

Unit time: 75 minutes

Complete this unit, and you'll know how to:

A Apply built-in and custom number formats to display data in specific formats.

B Use the UPPER, LOWER, PROPER, and SUBSTITUTE functions to modify text.

C Create, apply, and modify styles to apply several kinds of formatting simultaneously.

D Apply and modify themes.

E Merge and change orientation of cells to display text in special ways; transpose data; and add backgrounds and watermarks

Topic A: Using special number formats

This topic covers the following Microsoft Certified Application Specialist exam objective for Excel 2007.

#	Objective
2.3.2	Create custom cell formats

Built-in and custom formats

Explanation

You can apply special number formats—such as ZIP codes and phone numbers—to change the appearance of numerical information. You can do this by using built-in formats or by creating your own custom formats. You can also show or hide zeros in the worksheet.

Applying special number formats

When you apply a special number format to data in your worksheets, Excel changes only the cell's appearance and not the cell's value. So, when you click a cell where a number format has been applied, the formula bar still displays the unformatted value. Exhibit 2-1 shows part of a worksheet where built-in number formats have been applied to ZIP codes and phone numbers.

To apply a special format:

1. In the Format Cells dialog box, activate the Number tab, shown in Exhibit 2-2.
2. From the Category list, select Special.
3. From the Type list, select a format type. Click OK.

City	ZIP code	Name	Phone number
Ashford	06278	Bill MacArthur	(907) 345-4024
Georgetown	80444	Jamie Morrison	(800) 228-1425
Elbert	80106	Maureen O'Connor	(520) 284-0767
Farmington	06032	Rebecca Austin	(635) 565-4581
North Franklin	06254	Paul Anderson	(357) 613-2978
North Grosvenordale	06255	Cynthia Roberts	(526) 563-2440
North Windham	06256	Rita Greg	(246) 344-6657

Exhibit 2-1: The Number formats worksheet with special formats applied to two columns

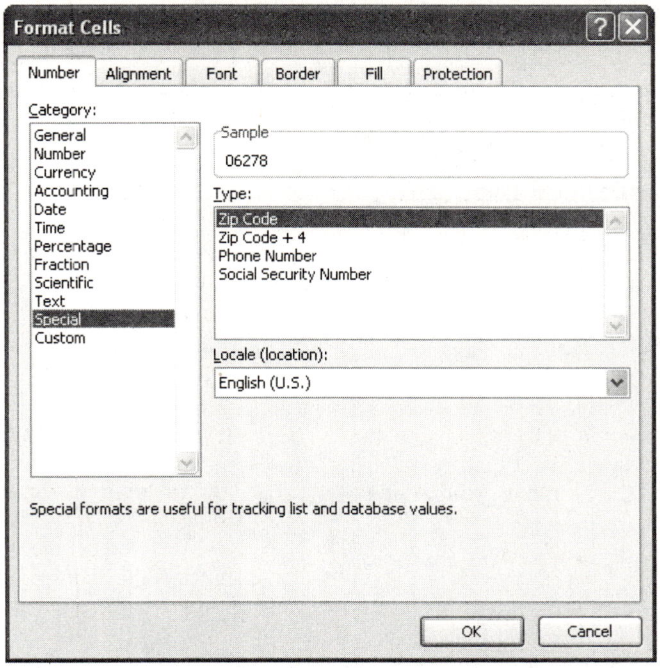

Exhibit 2-2: The Number tab in the Format Cells dialog box

Do it!

A-1: Applying special formats

Here's how	Here's why
1 Open Advanced formatting	In the current unit folder.
Save the workbook as **My advanced formatting**	
2 Verify that the Number formats worksheet is active	This worksheet contains the award details for managers.
3 Select B5:B23	The ZIP code column contains four- and five-digit ZIP codes. You'll apply the Zip Code format to this range to make sure that all ZIP codes contain five digits.
4 In the Number group, click	(The Dialog Box Launcher button is on the Home tab.) To open the Format Cells dialog box. The Number tab is active because you launched the dialog box from within the Number group.
From the Category list, select **Special**	The Special category includes formats for ZIP codes, phone numbers, and Social Security numbers. In the Type list, Zip Code is selected, as shown in Exhibit 2-2.
Click **OK**	To close the dialog box and apply the format.
5 Deselect the cells	The ZIP code values have been reformatted. Each four-digit value now begins with zero so that the value will conform to ZIP-code format.
6 Apply the Phone Number format to D5:D23	Select the range. In the Number group, click the Dialog Box Launcher to open the Format Cells dialog box with the Number tab active. From the Category list, select Special; then select Phone Number and click OK.
7 Select D5	
Observe the formula bar	 The cell value remains the same even though you have changed its display format in the worksheet.
8 Update the workbook	

Zero values

Explanation

Excel displays all zero values in a worksheet by default. However, if you prefer, you can hide zero values. To do so:

1 Click the Office Button and then click Excel Options.
2 Select Advanced.
3 Under "Display options for this worksheet," clear "Show a zero in cells that have a zero value."
4 Click OK.

Do it!

A-2: Controlling the display of zero values

Here's how	Here's why
1 Observe the worksheet	The Excellence awards and Gold medals columns contain several zero values.
2 Click 	
Click **Excel Options**	To open the Excel Options dialog box.
From the category list, select **Advanced**	
3 Under "Display options for this worksheet," clear the indicated option	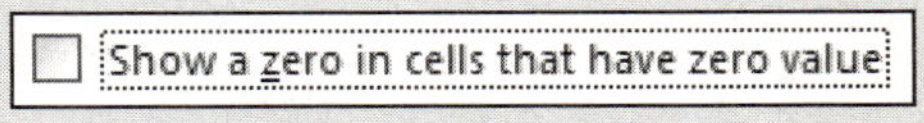 To hide zero values in this worksheet.
Click **OK**	To close the Excel Options dialog box.
4 Observe F5:G23	The cells that contained zero values earlier are now blank.
5 Update the workbook	

Custom number formats

Explanation

In Excel, you can create custom formats in which you specify the appearance of positive numbers, negative numbers, zero values, and text data.

To create a custom number format:

1 Activate the Number tab in the Format Cells dialog box, shown in Exhibit 2-3.
2 From the Category list, select Custom.
3 In the Type box, enter the desired format code.
4 Click OK to apply the format.

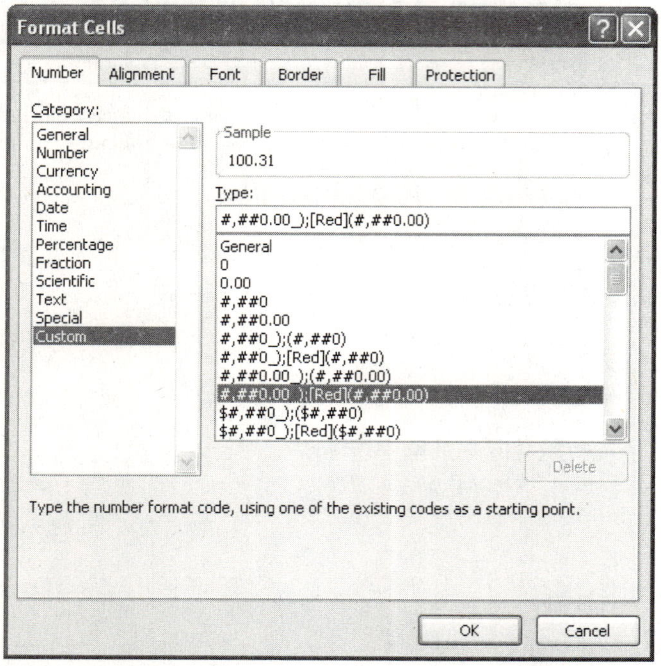

Exhibit 2-3: The Custom category in the Number tab of the Formatting Cells dialog box

A custom *format code* contains four sections—positives, negatives, zeros, and text—separated by semicolons. The syntax for all format codes is:

```
positive;negative;zero;text
```

The first section specifies how a positive value will appear in a cell. In the negative section, you can specify how a negative value should appear in a cell. The zero section controls the display of zero values, and the text section controls the appearance of text data. You can skip a section by entering consecutive semicolons.

Here's an example:

```
#,###.00_);[Red](#,###.00);0.00;"text"@
```

The `#` and `0` (zero) symbols are placeholders for digits. By using these symbols, you can specify how a numeric value should appear in a cell.

- In the positive section of the example, the code `#,###.00` means that positive numbers should have a comma in every thousandths position and have two digits after the decimal point.
- The underscore (_) adds a space that's the width of the character following it. In the example, negative numbers are enclosed in parentheses. Therefore, in the positive section, the underscore is followed by a closing parenthesis so that the positive numbers line up correctly with the negative numbers.
- In the negative section, `[Red]` indicates that all negative values will appear in the color red.
- In the zero section, `0.00` means that any zeros in the range would be shown in that format.
- The at symbol (`@`) displays a text value in a cell. You can identify specific text to be added automatically at the beginning of a text value; to do so, enclose that text in double quotes before the `@` symbol.

Exhibit 2-4 shows the effects of some of these format codes.

Name	City	Emp #	Gold medals	Last year	This year	% Increase
Bill MacArthur	Ashford	Empl: 17-111	1	$67,678	$135,567	100.31
Jamie Morrison	Georgetown	Empl: 46-721		$76,576	$65,737	(14.15)
Jim Adams	Elbert	Empl: 42-499		$114,867	$114,688	(0.16)
Rebecca Austin	Farmington	Empl: 42-617		$76,357	$86,548	13.35
Paul Anderson	North Franklin	Empl: 46-110		$85,566	$89,076	4.10
Cynthia Roberts	North Grosvenordale	Empl: 13-330		$39,076	$56,546	44.71
Rita Greg	North Windham	Empl: 42-220		$78,678	$67,888	(13.71)
Trevor Johnson	Elizabeth	Empl: 13-631		$64,874	$87,688	35.17
Kevin Meyers	Franktown	Empl: 46-551	3	$85,559	$184,888	116.09
Adam Long	Bennett	Empl: 13-668		$75,770	$85,665	13.06
Kendra James	Quinebaug	Empl: 13-235		$65,578	$55,786	(14.93)
Michael Lee	Rogers	Empl: 42-985		$69,867	$78,798	12.78
Sandra Lawrence	Scotland	Empl: 46-330	1	$76,377	$129,867	70.03
[illegible]	[illegible]	[illegible]		[illegible]	[illegible]	[illegible]

Exhibit 2-4: The Custom format worksheet after custom formats have been applied

Do it!

A-3: Creating custom formats

Here's how	Here's why
1 Activate the Custom format worksheet	This worksheet contains performance details for managers. You'll make the values in the % Increase column easier to interpret.
2 Select G5:G23	These cells contain positive and negative values.
Open the Format Cells dialog box	(Click the Dialog Box Launcher in the Number group.) The Number tab is active.
3 From the Category list, select **Custom**	To display the types of Custom formats.
From the Type list, select **#,##0.00_);[Red](#,##0.00)** as shown in Exhibit 2-3	
Click **OK**	To close the dialog box and apply the format.
4 Deselect the range	The values in the % Increase column are rounded to two decimal places. Negative values appear in red.
5 Select D5:D23	You'll hide the zeros in the Gold medals column.
6 Open the Format Cells dialog box	
From the Category list, select **Custom**	
Edit the Type box to read **0;-0;;@**	(This format is not in the Type list, so you must enter it in the Type box.) Here, ";;" indicates that the zeros section in the format code is empty; therefore, zeros will not be displayed. The @ symbol specifies that the cells in the range can accept and display text values.
Click **OK**	The cells containing zero values are now blank.
7 Select C5:C23	You'll add a prefix to all the values in this column and hyphenate the values.
8 Open the Format Cells dialog box	
From the Category list, select **Custom**	

9 Edit the Type box to read **"Empl: "00-000**	
Click **OK**	The prefix "Empl:", followed by a space, appears before all values in the Employee number column.
10 Update the workbook	

Topic B: Using functions to format text

This topic covers the following Microsoft Certified Application Specialist exam objectives for Excel 2007.

#	Objective
1.3.1	**Cut, copy, and paste data and cell contents** • Paste values instead of the formula
3.7.1	**Using PROPER, UPPER, LOWER, SUBSTITUTE**

The PROPER, UPPER, and LOWER functions

Explanation

In Excel, you can use a function to format text in a cell, and copy the result to a range of cells. This is more efficient than manually formatting each cell individually. For example, let's say you wanted to make all the names in a contact list uppercase. You could manually edit each name, but it would be much easier to use the UPPER function and copy the result to the cells you want to change.

Text-formatting functions include, but are not limited to, UPPER, LOWER, and PROPER. The syntax for these three functions is similar. It's the function name followed by `(text)`, like this—

```
UPPER(text)
```

—where `text` is the text you want to convert. It can refer to a cell or a text string.

Do it!

B-1: Using PROPER, UPPER, and LOWER

Here's how	Here's why
1 Activate the Text functions worksheet	You'll apply functions to format the text in this worksheet.
2 Select H4	
Enter **=PROPER(A4)**	To designate the text in A4 as the text you want to capitalize. Proper nouns, which include people's names, are generally capitalized.
Observe the screen	The first and last names in A4 now also appear in H4, but with each name starting with a capital letter.
3 Copy the formula in H4 to H5:H21	(Use the fill handle.) All names in the first column are capitalized.
4 Copy H4:H21	(Right-click the selection and choose Copy.) You'll paste the results of the function into the Name column.
Select A4:A21	
5 Right-click the selection and choose **Paste Special...**	To open the Paste Special dialog box.
Under Paste, select **Values**	To paste only the values, not the formulas.
Click **OK**	To close the dialog box and replace the list with capitalized names.
6 Press ESC	To delete the marquee around H4:H21.
Delete the values in H4:H21	You'll use this column to convert text in other columns.
7 Select H4	
Enter **=UPPER(F4)**	To convert the text in F4 to uppercase.
8 Copy the formula in H4 to H5:H21	
Replace the values in F4:F21 with the values in H4:H21	Copy the values in H4:H21 to F4:F21, using the Paste Special command.
Delete the contents of H4:H21	
9 Convert the text in G4:G21 to lowercase	Use the LOWER function. Be sure to delete the values from H4:H21 when you're done.
10 Update the workbook	

The SUBSTITUTE function

You can use the SUBSTITUTE function when you want to replace one character or set of characters with another set. The syntax for the SUBSTITUTE function is:

```
SUBSTITUTE(text,old_text,new_text,instance_num)
```

In this syntax, `text` is the text or cell reference for which you want to substitute new characters; `old_text` lists the characters you want to replace; and `new_text` is the text you want to substitute. `Instance_num` specifies which occurrence of `old_text` you want to replace with `new_text`.

Do it!

B-2: Using SUBSTITUTE

Here's how	Here's why
1 Observe the names in the Name column	Some letters in the last names should be capitalized, as in "MacArthur." You'll use SUBSTITUTE to correct this.
2 Select H4 Enter the following code: `=SUBSTITUTE(A4,"a","A",2)`	
	In this function, A4 is the cell containing the text to be replaced; "a" is the character to be replaced; and "A" is the replacement character. The 2 refers to the occurrence of the text to be replaced—that is, the second "a" in "Macarthur."
3 Copy the result from H4 to A4	Use the Paste Special command to copy only the value in H4, not the formula.
4 In H4, enter the following code: `=SUBSTITUTE(A6,"g","G",1)` Copy the result to A6	To correct Melinda's McGregor's last name.
5 Delete the contents of H4 Update the workbook	

Topic C: Working with styles

This topic covers the following Microsoft Certified Application Specialist exam objective for Excel 2007.

#	Objective
2.3.3	**Apply and modify cell styles** • Format cells by using Quick Styles

Benefits of styles

Explanation

You might want to apply several formats at the same time. You can do this efficiently by creating a style that has all the formats you want to use and then applying that style to the cell or range. A *style* is a named collection of formats that are saved and applied as a group.

Creating and applying styles

Excel provides a gallery of built-in cell styles, also called Quick Styles. You can also create and modify your own styles to make data appear exactly as you want.

Built-in styles

You can view a gallery of built-in styles by clicking Cell Styles in the Styles group on the Home tab. When you point to a style in the gallery, the Live Preview function in Excel 2007 temporarily applies that style to whatever cell or range is selected. If you click a style, it is applied to the selected cell, and the gallery closes. The Cell Styles gallery is shown in Exhibit 2-5.

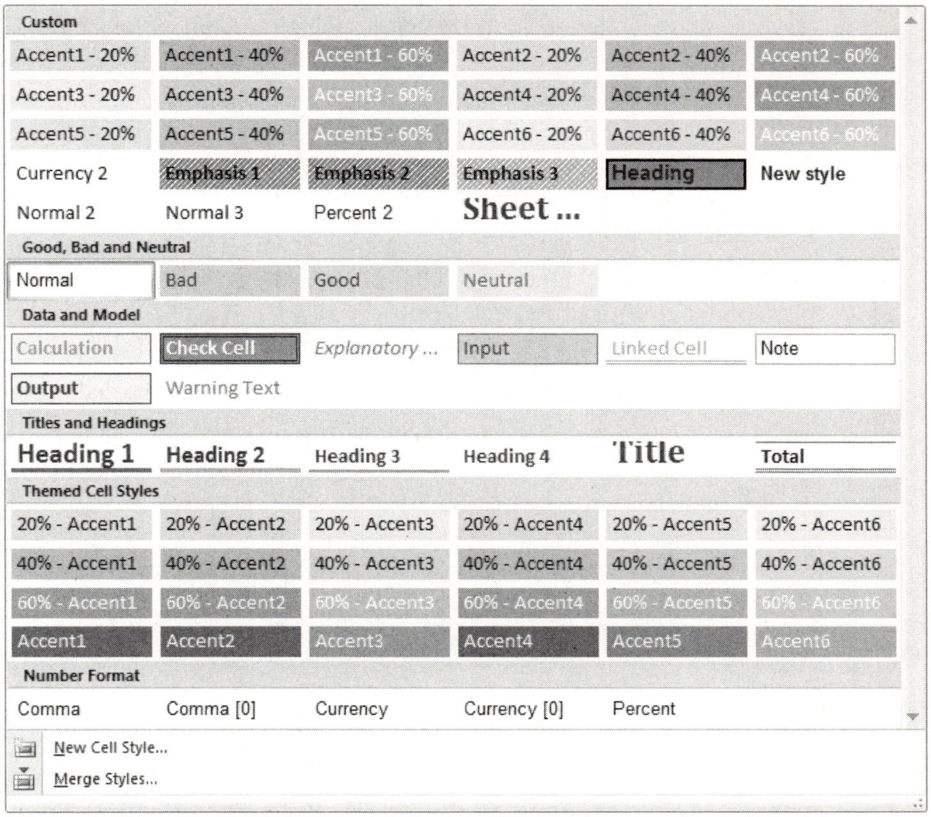

Exhibit 2-5: The Cell Styles gallery

Custom styles

You can also create your own styles that combine formats in any way you want. To create a custom style:

1. Select a cell that already has the combination of formats you want to include in the new style.
2. Activate the Home tab.
3. In the Styles group, click Cell Styles to display the gallery.
4. Choose New Cell Style (near the bottom of the gallery) to open the Style dialog box, shown in Exhibit 2-6. The dialog box shows the combination of formats from the selected cell.
5. In the Style name box, enter a name for the new style.
6. Click OK to define the new style and close the dialog box.

After you create a style, the Style gallery will be divided into Custom and Built-In styles. The style you created will appear in the Custom section, near the top of the gallery.

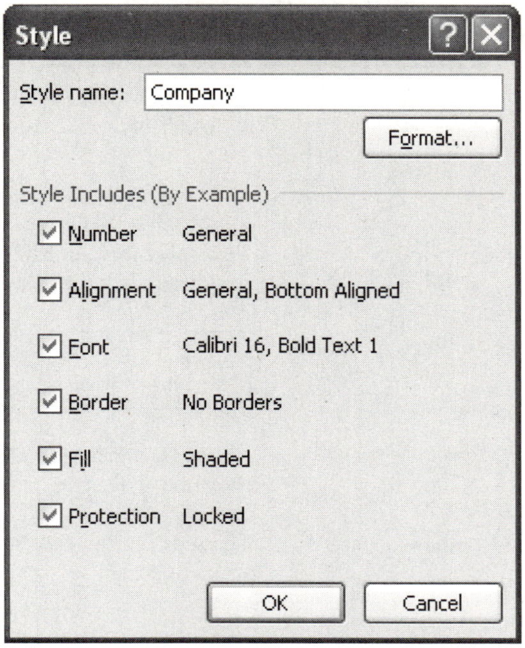

Exhibit 2-6: The Style dialog box showing the new style Company

Do it!

C-1: Creating and applying styles

Here's how	Here's why
1 Activate the Custom format worksheet	You'll use Live Preview to view some built-in styles; then you'll create custom styles.
Select B13	
2 In the Styles group, click **Cell Styles**	To display the Cell Styles gallery. The gallery contains only built-in styles at this time.
In the Cell Styles gallery, point as shown	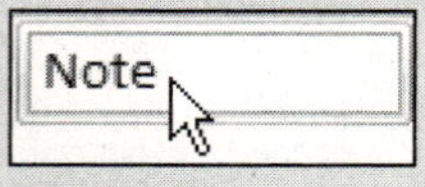 (In the Data and Model group.) B13 changes to show the Note style, with yellow shading.
Point to the other styles in the gallery	To see Live Preview temporarily apply the styles to B13.
3 Select A1	You'll create a style based on the format of A1.
Click **Cell Styles**	To display the Cell Styles gallery.
Choose **New Cell Style...**	To open the Style dialog box.
4 Edit the Style name box to read **Company**	To name the new style, as shown in Exhibit 2-6. Under Style Includes (By Example), the formatting options of the new style are checked. These are drawn from the format of the selected cell (A1).
Click **OK**	To finish creating the Company style and to close the dialog box.
5 Select G6	You'll create a style based on the format of G6.
6 Open the Style dialog box	In the Styles group, click Cell Styles; then choose New Cell Style.
Edit the Style name box to read **NegativeNum**	
Under Style Includes (By Example), clear **Border**	To ensure that the style, when applied, does not change the borders of the target cell(s).
Click **OK**	To create the NegativeNum style and close the dialog box.
7 Create a style named **ColumnHeading** based on A4	Select the cell. In the Styles group, click Cell Styles; then choose New Cell Style. Edit the Style name box to read ColumnHeading and click OK.

8	Create a style named **Title2** based on A2	The gallery already has a Title style.
9	Activate the Styles worksheet	You'll apply the styles you created to the data in this worksheet.
10	Select A1:C1	
11	Open the Cell Styles gallery	(In the Styles group, click Cell Styles.) There is now a Custom group at the top of the gallery.
	Under Custom, select **Company**	To apply the new style to the selected range. A1:C1 has been reformatted.
12	Apply the Title2 style to A2:C2	Open the Cell Styles gallery and select Title2.
13	Apply the Column heading style to A4:E4	
14	Apply the NegativeNum style to E5:E23	
15	Update the workbook	

Modifying built-in or custom styles

Explanation

To modify a style (built-in or custom):

1. Open the Cell Styles gallery and point to the style you want to modify.
2. Right-click and choose Modify to open the Style dialog box.
3. Clear the check boxes for any formats you want to remove from the style.
4. If you want to add or change formats, then click Format to open the Format Cells dialog box. Make your changes and click OK.
5. Click OK to close the Style dialog box.

Do it!

C-2: Modifying styles

Here's how	Here's why
1 Select E5	If necessary.
2 Open the Cell Styles gallery	You'll modify the NegativeNum style you created earlier.
Right-click **NegativeNum** and choose **Modify...**	To open the Style dialog box. Under Style includes, the checked boxes indicate the formats that make up this style.
Click **Format**	To open the Format Cells dialog box. You can use this dialog box to modify any style (built-in or custom).
3 Activate the Number tab	If necessary.
Under Category, select **Number**	If necessary.
4 Edit the Decimal places box to read **1**	To specify that values displayed with the NegativeNum style will have only one digit to the right of the decimal point.
From the Negative numbers list, select the indicated format	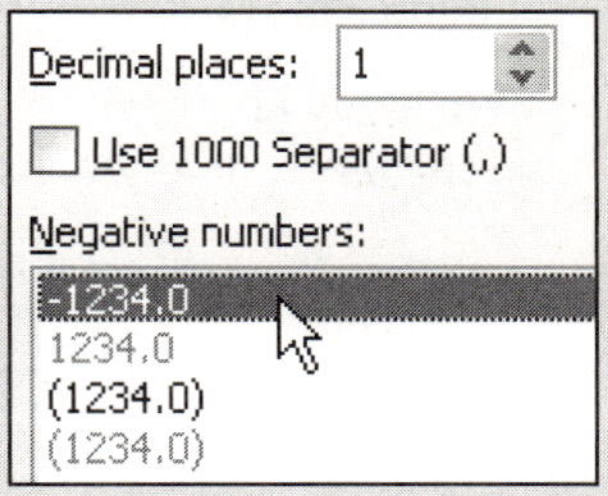 To specify that negative values displayed with the NegativeNum style will appear in black, preceded by a minus (-) sign.
Click **OK**	To close the Format Cells dialog box and return to the Style dialog box.
5 Click **OK**	To close the Style dialog box and apply the modified NegativeNum style.
6 Observe E5:E23	All cells in this range use the NegativeNum style. The values in this range now appear with only one decimal place. Negative numbers appear in black, preceded by a minus (-) sign.
7 Update the workbook	

Topic D: Working with themes

This topic covers the following Microsoft Certified Application Specialist exam objective for Excel 2007.

#	Objective
2.1.1	**Use themes to format worksheets** • Apply a theme to a workbook • Modify and save a theme

Benefits of themes

Explanation

At times, you might want to change some of the colors or fonts you've used in a workbook, or even in several workbooks. You could change elements individually as they appear in each sheet, but that would be tedious and time-consuming. Instead, you can use Excel's themes to swap each instance of a specific color or font with another or to quickly replace the entire color scheme.

Theme colors

When you apply colors in Excel, you can use theme colors, standard colors, recently used colors, or any color you specify, as shown in Exhibit 2-7.

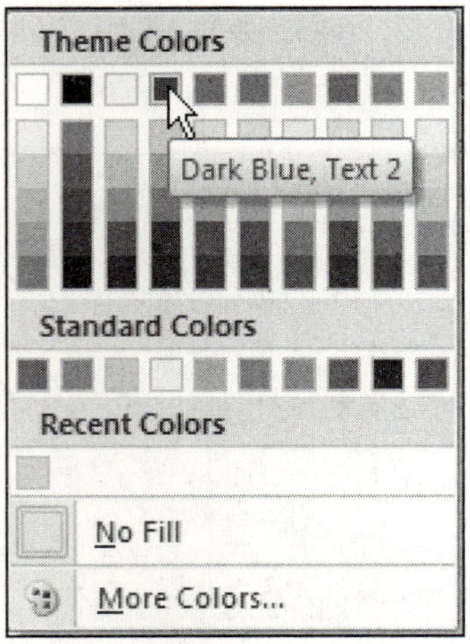

Exhibit 2-7: Color selection options

Choosing colors from the Theme Colors section of the gallery has several benefits:

- You can switch to a different theme to replace all of the theme colors at once. A theme change applies to all sheets within a workbook.
- Colors in built-in themes were selected to work harmoniously. It's easy to select complementary colors from the theme colors, whereas selecting custom colors can result in clashing combinations.
- If you apply the first four Text/Background colors—with dark text on light backgrounds, and light text on dark backgrounds—for their intended purposes, and then switch themes, the text will probably still be legible regardless of the theme you change to. This is because all of the default themes that come with Office 2007 position the dark and light colors in the same positions within the theme. So, a theme change could switch from white text on dark blue to very light gray text on dark green—but not to navy blue text on black, which would be hard to read.
- Each theme color appears in several *tints*, or brightness variations. For a simple but effective look, you can juxtapose light and dark tints of the same color (for example, placing dark blue text in a cell filled with light blue).

Applying themes

In addition to controlling colors, each theme also controls fonts and effects. You can switch all of these attributes at once, or change just one of them.

To swap multiple colors, fonts, or effects by using themes:

1. Apply colors with the possibility of changing themes in mind:
   - Apply theme colors wherever you anticipate needing to change colors globally (throughout a workbook). Many built-in cell styles are formatted with theme colors for consistency.
   - For the most reliable text legibility when switching themes, use the first four colors for text and backgrounds, with contrasting combinations (light on dark or vice versa).
   - If you want certain colors *not* to change (for example, fill colors in cells you want to draw attention to), then use either standard colors or colors you define yourself, not theme colors.
2. Activate the Page Layout tab.
3. Change one or more theme attributes:
   - To change colors, fonts, and effects all at once, choose a theme from the Themes gallery in the Themes group.
   - To change colors, fonts, or effects individually, choose options from the corresponding menus in the Themes group.

Do it!

D-1: Changing to a different theme

Here's how	Here's why
1 Open Themes	
Save the workbook as **My themes**	You'll apply formatting with both theme and non-theme colors.
2 Select A2	You'll apply a cell style, which uses a theme color.
3 Open the Cell Styles gallery	
Under Titles and Headings, select **Heading 1**	To apply the Heading 1 style.
Observe the font color applied	(Click the Font Color gallery in the Font group and observe the color with the box around it.) This text has been formatted with the Dark Blue, Text 2 color.
4 From the Fill Color gallery in the Font group, select the indicated color	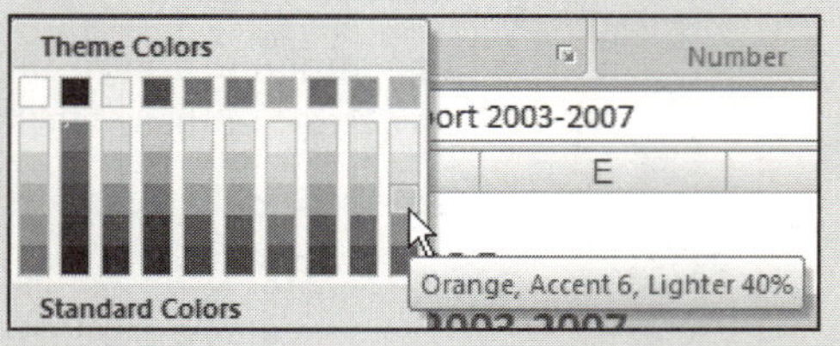 To apply an accent color that will change when you change themes. You'll select some contrasting type and background colors for the table headings and body.
5 Select B4:F4	
Hold CTRL and select A5:A9	To select the two non-contiguous ranges simultaneously.
From the Fill Color gallery in the Font group, select Dark Blue, Text 2	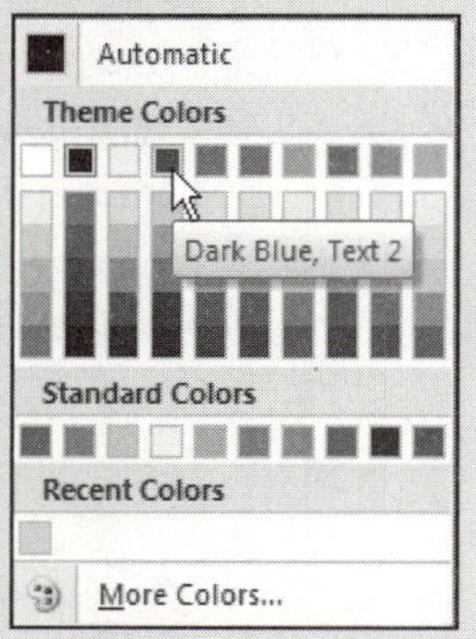
From the Font Color list in the Font group, select White, Background 1	To create contrasting type for the dark background.

6	Select B5:F9	The values in the table.
	From the Fill Color list in the Font group, select Tan, Background 2	To fill the table body with a light color. Next, you'll highlight a cell that represents good growth from the prior year.
7	Fill D9 with a green color under Standard colors	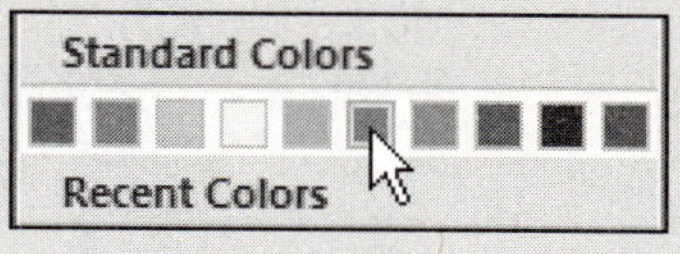 To apply a contrasting color that won't change when you change themes.
	Activate the Profit projection sheet	To observe that this sheet was already formatted with many of the same colors. You'll change themes to change the entire color scheme for both sheets in one step.
8	Activate the Page Layout tab	
9	In the Themes group, click **Themes**	To open the Themes gallery.
10	Point to several themes to see the effect on the colors and fonts in the worksheet	Colors and fonts change to reflect the colors and fonts each theme would apply.
11	Point to the Civic theme	The table text remains legible, but the text in A2 is harder to read. This demonstrates that the Text/Background color choices are safe for legibility when you change themes, but type over accent colors might be hard to read when another theme is applied.
12	Select the Origin theme	This theme applies muted, conservative colors and fonts typically appropriate for financial reporting. However, the red color in B9 remains because it is a standard color, not a theme color.
13	Activate the Sales Report sheet	The colors were applied to all sheets in the workbook. The green color you applied to D9 remains because it is not a theme color.
14	Update the workbook	

Defining theme colors

Explanation

In addition to applying themes in their entirety, you can use the Create New Theme Colors dialog box, shown in Exhibit 2-8, to define your own sets of colors. You can save just the colors, or an entire new theme, to create a formatting scheme that fits your organization's identity.

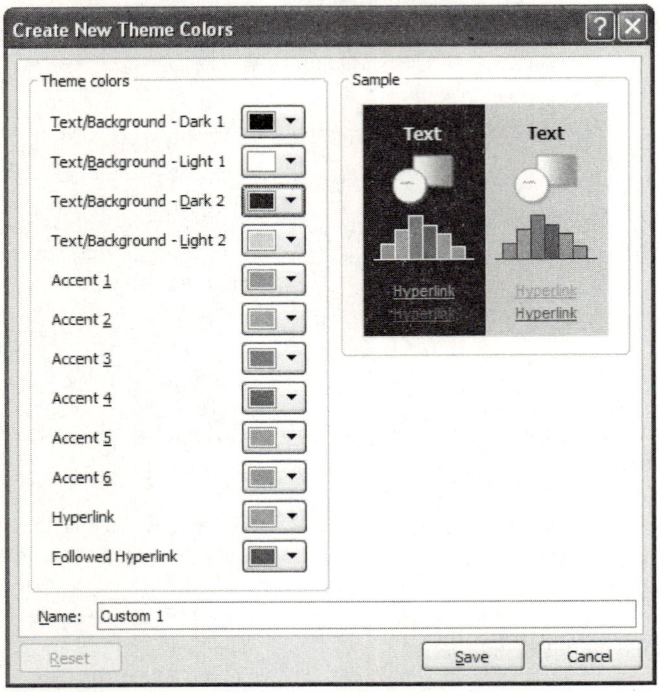

Exhibit 2-8: The Create New Theme Colors dialog box

To create a new set of theme colors:

1. Activate the Page Layout tab.
2. In the Themes group, from the Colors menu, choose Create New Theme Colors.
3. Change one or more of the theme colors. To do so, click the button for the color you want to change, and then do one of the following:
   - Select one of the other theme colors (although this would create some redundant colors in the palette).
   - Select one of the standard colors.
   - Click More Colors to open the Colors dialog box, and use it to select or define a color from millions of possibilities.
4. In the Name box, enter a name for the new set of theme colors.
5. Click Save.

Changing and saving other theme attributes

In addition to altering colors within a theme, you can change fonts and effects. Choose fonts and effects from the lists in the Themes dialog box to apply them to the current workbook.

To save the current combination of colors, fonts, and effects as a theme, choose Save Current Theme from the Themes menu, enter a name, and click Save.

Do it!

D-2: Saving new colors and themes

Here's how	Here's why
1 In the Themes group, from the Colors gallery, choose **Create New Theme Colors...**	To open the Create New Theme Colors dialog box. You'll change the third Text/Background color to a dark blue to give the workbook a bit more color.
Click as shown	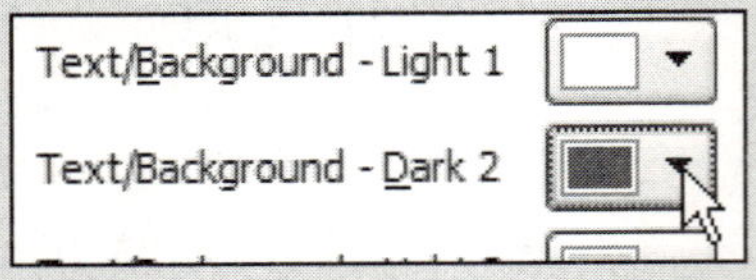 To display the palette for the Text/Background – Dark 2 theme color.
From the Standard colors, select **Dark Blue**	The second-to-last color.
2 Edit the Name box to read **My colors**	
Click **Save**	To close the dialog box and save the new theme colors. The text in the top two cells and the table heading cells is dark blue because those cells are formatted with the Text/Background - Dark 2 color.
3 In the Themes group, open the Colors gallery	You'll modify the theme colors you just created.
Under Custom, right-click **My colors**	To display a shortcut menu.
Choose **Edit...**	To open the Edit Theme Colors dialog box.
4 Click the arrow to the right of Text/Background – Dark 2	To display the color palette.
Choose **More Colors...**	To open the Colors dialog box.
Activate the Custom tab	(If necessary.) To display a more versatile interface for selecting colors than the Standard tab. Colors are represented numerically as amounts of Red, Green, and Blue (RGB) components. Each component can range in value from 0 (none of that component) to 255 (that component fully saturated). The higher the RGB component values, the brighter the color overall.

5	Drag the Brightness slider up until the Green value is approximately 50 and the Blue value is approximately 150, as shown	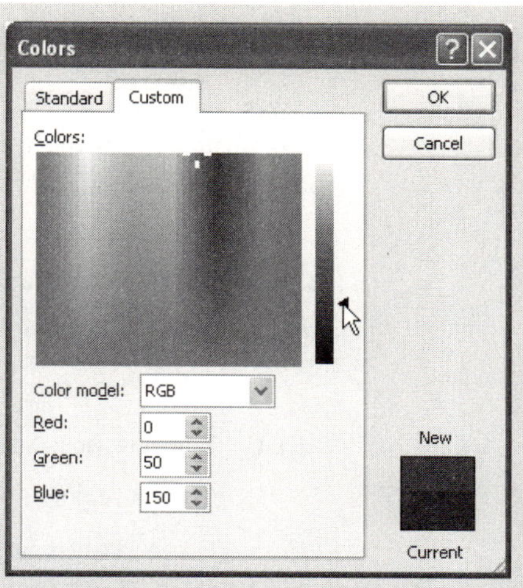
6	Click **OK**	To close the Colors dialog box.
	Click **Save**	To close the Edit Theme Colors dialog box and save the set of colors. Next, you'll change the default heading and body fonts.
7	In the Themes group, display the Fonts menu and choose **Flow**	To select a combination of Heading and Body fonts. These appear in the top two cells in this worksheet because the Sheet Title and Heading 1 cell styles specify the Heading and Body fonts.
8	From the Themes menu, choose **Save Current Theme...**	To open the Save Current Theme dialog box.
	In the File name box, enter **My theme**	
	Click **Save**	
9	From the Themes gallery, select another theme	(Any theme will do.) To change the formatting.
	From the Themes menu, under Custom, choose **My theme**	To reapply your formatting to the cells that specify theme colors and fonts.
10	Update and close the workbook	

Topic E: Other advanced formatting

This topic covers the following Microsoft Certified Application Specialist exam objectives for Excel 2007.

#	Objective
1.3.1	**Cut, copy, and paste data and cell contents** • Transpose data during paste
2.1.4	**Format worksheet backgrounds** • Add color • Add watermarks
2.3.6	**Merge and split cells**

Options for advanced worksheet formatting

Explanation

You can change the appearance of text in a worksheet in a variety of ways. You can merge cells, center cells, and use indents to align text within cells or within text boxes. You change the orientation of text, so it's displayed vertically in a cell. You can also transpose data when pasting, so that row data and column data are switched. Additionally, you can format the worksheet background by adding a picture or a watermark.

Merging cells

You can center text that extends across multiple cells by merging those cells into one. To do this, select the cells to be merged; then, in the Alignment group on the Home tab, click Merge & Center.

When you use the Merge & Center button to merge cells in a column or a row, the text is centered horizontally. You can use the vertical and horizontal alignment buttons in the Alignment group to change the position of text in a merged cell.

Indenting text in a merged cell

You can also indent text in merged cells. For example, you can indent text from the left by clicking the Increase Indent button in the Alignment group.

Do it!

E-1: Merging cells

Here's how	Here's why
1 Activate the Sales worksheet	(My advanced formatting should still be open.) You'll insert a table title in this worksheet.
2 Insert a column before column A	(Select column A, right-click, and choose Insert from the shortcut menu.) An Insert Options smart tag appears.
3 Select A5	
Enter **East and North regions**	The text is not completely visible.
4 Activate the Home tab	
5 Select A5:A17	
Click 	(The Merge & Center button is in the Alignment group.) The cells have been merged into one cell, but the text is still not completely visible. The text appears centered at the bottom of the cell. You'll correct this in the next activity.
6 Update the workbook	

Changing orientation of cell contents

Explanation

You can change the orientation of text in a cell, as shown in Exhibit 2-9. *Orientation* refers to the direction of text flow in a cell. By default, text is horizontal. You can also display it vertically or rotate it to a specific angle.

To do this, use the Orientation button in the Alignment group on the Home tab. To rotate text to a specific angle, open the Format Cells dialog box and enter a value between 0 and 90 degrees in the Degrees box on the Alignment tab. A preview of the angle is displayed for you.

East and North regions	Product	Region	January	February	March	April	Total
	Cinnamon (Ground Korintje)	East	$20,345	$29,196	$17,990	$18,158	$85,689
	Cinnamon (Ground) Extra High Oil (2X)	East	$26,400	$34,879	$15,541	$22,731	$99,551
	Anise Seeds	East	$2,253	$2,139	$11,312	$20,218	$35,923
	Annatto Seed	East	$2,146	$1,871	$11,771	$24,181	$39,969
	Asafoetida Powder	East	$18,772	$18,780	$19,426	$23,273	$80,251
	Sub total (East)		$69,916	$86,865	$76,039	$108,561	$341,381
	Basil Leaf (Whole)	North	$2,511	$2,158	$17,611	$25,166	$47,446
	Basil Leaf (Ground)	North	$3,829	$1,753	$17,314	$17,924	$40,820
	Cardamom Seed (Ground)	North	$3,190	$2,471	$17,975	$25,573	$49,209
	Carob Powder (Raw)	North	$3,248	$3,253	$13,839	$18,336	$38,676
	Carob Pods (Ribbled)	North	$2,301	$2,468	$17,648	$23,818	$46,235
	Sub total (North)		$15,079	$12,103	$84,388	$110,817	$222,387

Exhibit 2-9: Text in the first column is rotated up

Do it!

E-2: Changing the orientation of text in a cell

Here's how	Here's why
1 Select A5	(If necessary.) You'll change the orientation of text in the cell so that the title is completely visible.
2 In the Alignment group, click [Orientation button]	To display the Orientation menu.
Choose **Rotate Text Up**	To rotate the text 90 degrees.
Click [Middle Align button]	(The Middle Align button is in the Alignment group.) To center the text vertically in the cell.
3 Click **B**	(The Bold button is in the Font group.) To make the text bold. The text in A5 is now displayed vertically, centered in the merged cell, and bold, as shown in Exhibit 2-9.
4 Update the workbook	

Splitting merged cells

Explanation

After you have merged a range of cells, you might need to split them. To do so, select the merged cell, click the down-arrow on the Merge & Center button in the Alignment group, and choose Unmerge Cells.

Do it!

E-3: Splitting cells

Here's how — **Here's why**

1 Activate the Split cells worksheet

This worksheet contains the bonus sales report for four salespeople. The table title is merged and centered across the five columns containing the sales report. You'll add the bonus sales details for a fifth salesperson, and then split the cells containing the table title so that it extends over all six columns.

2 In F4, enter **Tina Ralls**

To enter the name of the fifth salesperson.

3 In F5:F8, enter data as shown

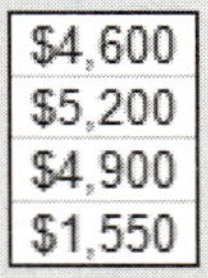

4 Apply and remove borders for the new column of data so that it matches the other columns, as shown

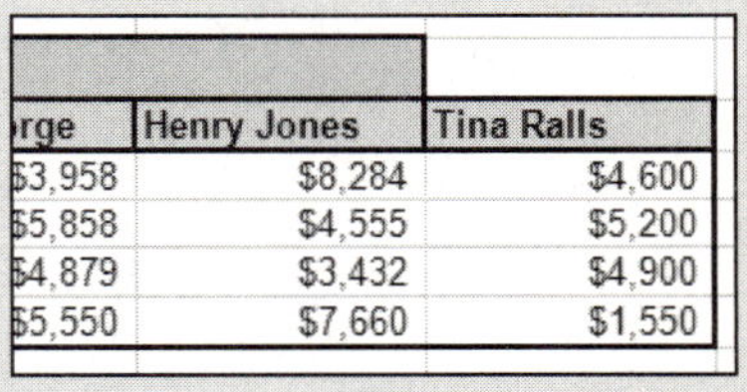

5 Select A3

The range A3:E3 is selected because the cells in this range are merged.

Click the down-arrow on the Merge & Center button and choose **UnMerge Cells**

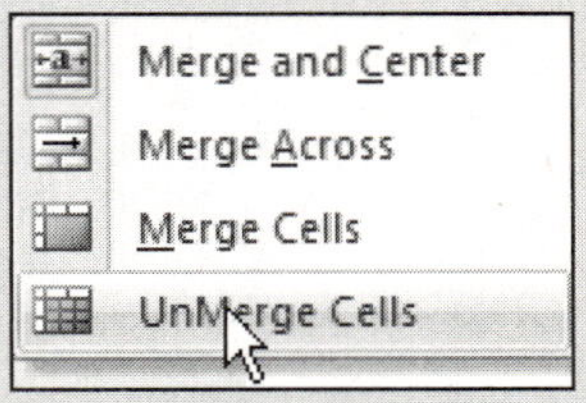

To split the cells in the range A3:E3.

6 Select A3:F3

You'll merge cells and center the table title across the new range.

Click 

The cells are merged, and the table title is centered across all six columns.

7 Update the workbook

Transposing data

Explanation

There may be times when you've entered data into rows that you should have put in columns, and vice versa. In Excel, you can quickly switch the placement of data in rows and columns by using the Transpose command.

The Transpose command is available as a Paste Special option. To transpose rows and columns:

1. Select the range whose layout you want to switch.
2. Copy the selected range. You must copy the selection rather than cutting it; otherwise, the Paste Special options will not be available.
3. Select the cell where you want to paste the copy.
4. From the Paste Special menu, choose Transpose.

Do it!

E-4: Transposing data during a paste

Here's how	Here's why
1 Activate the Transpose worksheet	You want the names to appear in the first column, rather than in the row they're in now.
2 Select A4:E8	
Right-click the selection and choose **Copy**	
3 Select A12	You'll paste the data here.
4 Click as shown	 To display the Paste Special menu.
Choose **Transpose**	To transpose the row and column data.
Press ESC	To turn off the marquee around A4:E8.
5 Adjust the column widths	To make all the data visible.
Update the workbook	

Adding backgrounds to a worksheet

Explanation

You can add interest to a worksheet by adding a background color. Simply select the cells whose background color you want to change, and choose a color from the Fill Color gallery.

In addition, you can insert a background graphic via the Background command. The Background command is available in the Page Setup group on the Page Layout tab. Unlike fill colors, however, background graphics do not print.

To add a background picture:

1. Activate the Page Layout tab.
2. In the Page Setup group, click Background to open the Sheet Background dialog box.
3. Select the desired background picture.
4. Click Insert.

Do it!

E-5: Adding and deleting backgrounds

Here's how	Here's why
1 Activate the Background sheet	
2 Select A1:F44	You'll add a background color to all the cells in this range.
3 Activate the Home tab	If necessary.
4 In the Font group, click the down-arrow on the Fill Color button	To open the Fill Color gallery.
Select the indicated color	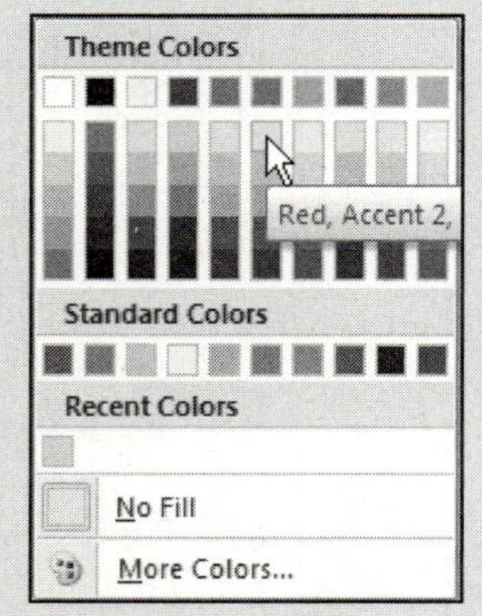 All cells in the range now have the same background color.
5 Select A4:E23	You'll apply a different background color to this range so that it stands out.
From the Fill Color gallery, select a light color	To change the background color of the selected cells.
6 Preview the page	The background colors you applied will print.
Close Print Preview	
7 Press  twice	To delete the background you just applied. You'll use the Background command to insert a background.
Deselect the range	
8 Activate the Page Layout tab	
In the Page Setup group, click **Background**	To open the Sheet Background dialog box.
Navigate to the current unit folder	If necessary.

9	Select **Background**	
	Click **Insert**	To insert the file as a picture in the worksheet's background. The background image can be seen through the data, making the data harder to read.
10	Add a light fill color to A4:E23	To set the range apart from the background image.
	Preview the page	The worksheet background is not visible because pictures used as backgrounds do not print.
	Close Print Preview	You'll delete the background picture.
11	Activate the Page Layout tab	
	In the Page Setup group, click **Delete Background**	To delete the background picture. This won't affect the fill color in A4:E23.
	Update the workbook	

Adding watermarks

Explanation

A watermark is a printable graphic often added to documents to convey an attribute such as confidentiality or document ownership. Although Excel does not have a watermark feature, you can mimic a watermark by adding a picture to a section of a header or footer.

To mimic a watermark in a worksheet:

1. Activate the Insert tab.
2. In the Text group, click Header & Footer. The Header & Footer Tools appear, adding a Design tab to the Ribbon.
3. Click in the header or footer section where you want to insert the watermark picture.
4. On the Design tab, in the Header and Footer Elements group, click Picture to open the Insert Picture dialog box.
5. Select a picture and click Insert.

Do it!

E-6: Adding a watermark

Here's how	Here's why
1 Activate the Insert tab	
In the Text group, click **Header & Footer**	To switch to Print Layout view, with the center header section selected. The Header & Footer Tools | Design tab is active.
Click the right header section	You'll insert a watermark picture here.
2 In the Header & Footer Elements group, click **Picture**	To open the Insert Picture dialog box.
Navigate to the current unit folder	If necessary.
3 Select **Confidential**	
Click **Insert**	To insert the picture.
4 Deselect the header section	Click any cell in the body of the worksheet. The new picture appears.
5 Update and close the workbook	

Unit summary: Advanced formatting

Topic A In this topic, you learned how to apply **special number formats** to ZIP codes, Social Security numbers, and phone numbers. You learned how to hide or display **zero values** in an entire worksheet and in a selected range. You also learned how to use **custom formats** to display data in specific formats.

Topic B In this topic, you learned how to use functions to **format text**. You learned how to use UPPER, LOWER, and PROPER to change the case of text. You also learned how to use the SUBSTITUTE function to change one text character to another.

Topic C In this topic, you learned about the **built-in styles** that Excel provides. Then, you learned how to create and apply styles. You also learned how to modify styles.

Topic D In this topic, you learned about the various **themes** that Excel provides. You learned how to apply and modify themes.

Topic E In this topic, you learned how to **merge cells**, change the **orientation** of text within cells, and **split** merged cells. You also learned how to **transpose** data during a paste operation. Finally, you learned how to add **backgrounds** and mimic **watermarks** in a worksheet.

Independent practice activity

In this activity, you'll create styles and apply them to other worksheets. You'll merge and center cells and use a function to format text. Then you'll apply a number format and add a watermark.

1 Open Practice advanced formatting and save it as **My practice advanced formatting**. Verify that the Practice advanced formatting worksheet is active.

2 Create custom styles called **Company**, **Title1**, **Column heading**, and **Region** based on the current worksheet. Apply these styles to the Apply styles worksheet.

3 Merge and center the company name and the subtitle over the entire width of the data.

4 Use the PROPER function to capitalize the employee names as proper nouns.

5 Format the data in column D with a phone-number format. Compare your results to Exhibit 2-10.

6 Insert the Confidential watermark picture in the left footer section.

7 Update and close the workbook.

Outlander Spices			
Employee contract details			
Region	Name	Emp #	Phone number
East	Pamela Carter	17121	(907) 345-4024
East	Anna Morris	46321	(800) 228-1425
East	Rita Lawson	42449	(520) 284-0767
East	Sam Peters	42517	(635) 565-4581
North	Julie George	46160	(357) 613-2978
North	Diana Stone	13337	(526) 563-2440
South	Rob Dukes	42820	(246) 344-6657
South	Tammy Heiret	13691	(545) 454-5457
South	Sandy Stewart	46550	(632) 653-5235
South	Wendy Alto	13168	(677) 376-3760
South	Tina Ralls	13225	(327) 567-6636
West	Nikki Cleary	42983	(523) 436-6373
West	Davis Lee	46430	(527) 786-7872
West	David Ford	46950	(633) 646-4643
West	Julia Stockton	46343	(545) 865-6544
West	Sonia McCormick	13641	(774) 777-4383

Exhibit 2-10: The Apply Styles worksheet after Step 5

Review questions

1 List the steps to apply a special number format.

2 When you apply special number formats to data, Excel changes both the cell's appearance and the cell's value. True or false?

3 What is one way to control the display of zero values in a cell?

4 What is a style?

5 Can you apply a watermark to an Excel spreadsheet?

Unit 3
Outlining and subtotals

Unit time: 45 minutes

Complete this unit, and you'll know how to:

A Create outlines to group and organize data, and consolidate data from different worksheets.

B Summarize the data in a worksheet by creating automatic subtotals.

Topic A: Outlining and consolidating data

This topic covers the following Microsoft Certified Application Specialist exam objective for Excel 2007.

#	Objective
4.5.1	Group and ungroup data

Options for grouping data

Explanation

You can organize data in a worksheet by creating an outline. An outline groups data by levels. Each level contains a section of the data that you can expand or collapse. A worksheet can have up to eight levels of detail. You can also consolidate data from different worksheets to summarize the data.

Outlining

To outline data:

1. Select the range of cells for which you want to create an outline.
2. Verify that the summary rows or columns you want to outline are located in the same position relative to the detailed data. For example, the summary columns might be located either to the right or to the left of the detailed data, but not in both positions.
3. Activate the Data tab.
4. In the Outline group, click the down-arrow beside Group and choose Auto Outline.

After creating an outline, you can use the outline symbols to expand and collapse data, as shown in Exhibit 3-1 and Exhibit 3-2. You can also expand or collapse data by row or column level. You can click the lowest-level button to show all details, and click the highest-level button to hide all details. (The higher the number, the lower the outline level.) For example, if an outline has four levels, click 4 to show details of all four levels, and click 1 to hide all details.

Selecting a large range

When using a large worksheet, you might need to select a range that covers several screens. It can be difficult to select this range by dragging. Another way to select such a range is to click the first cell in the range, press and hold Shift, and click the last cell in the range.

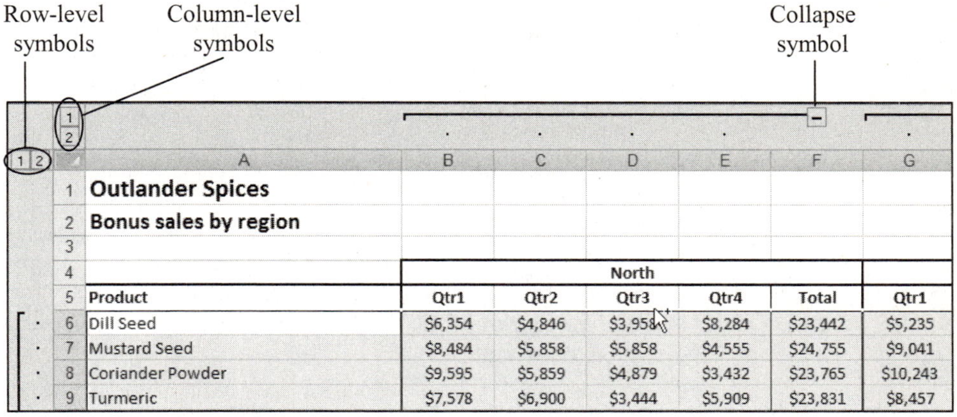

Exhibit 3-1: The expanded form

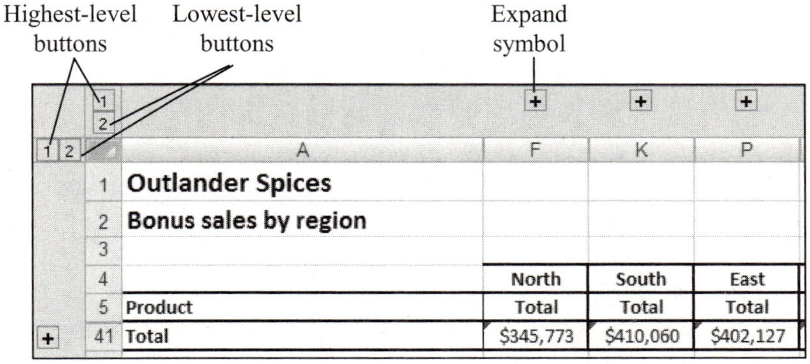

Exhibit 3-2: The collapsed form

Do it!

A-1: Creating an outline

Here's how	Here's why
1 Open Outlining	(In the current unit folder.) The Quarterly sales worksheet contains more rows and columns than can typically be displayed when viewed at 100% magnification. You'll create an outline that displays only aggregate sales figures.
Save the workbook as **My outlining**	In the current unit folder.
2 Select A6	To select the first cell in a range.
Press and hold SHIFT and select Z41	To select the range A6:Z41.
Release SHIFT	
3 Activate the Data tab	
In the Outline group, click as shown	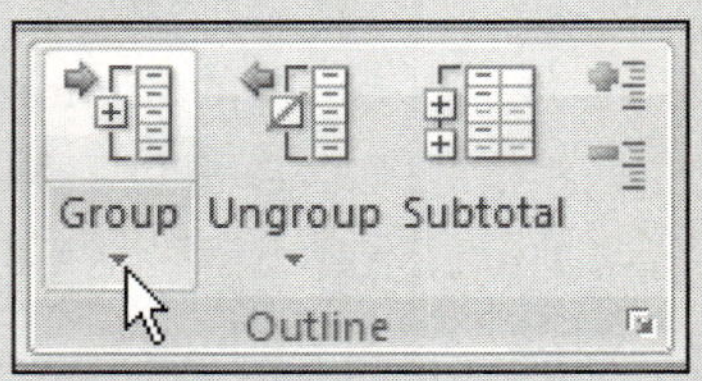 To display the Group menu.
Choose **Auto Outline**	To outline the selected data. Various symbols appear above and to the left of the worksheet.
4 Click the collapse symbol above column F, as shown	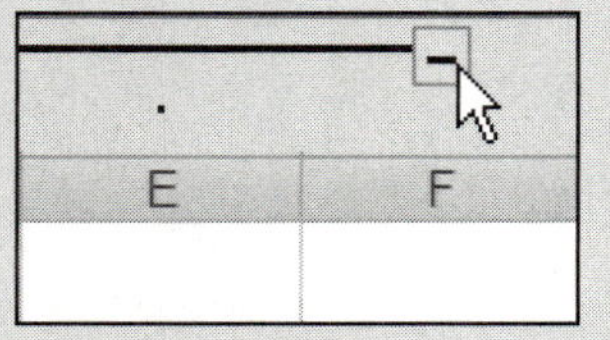 (The collapse symbol resembles a minus sign.) To collapse the quarterly sales data for the North region and show only the total sales. There is now an expand symbol (+) above column F. The quarterly sales columns for the other regions are still visible.

5 Collapse the quarterly sales data for the other regions

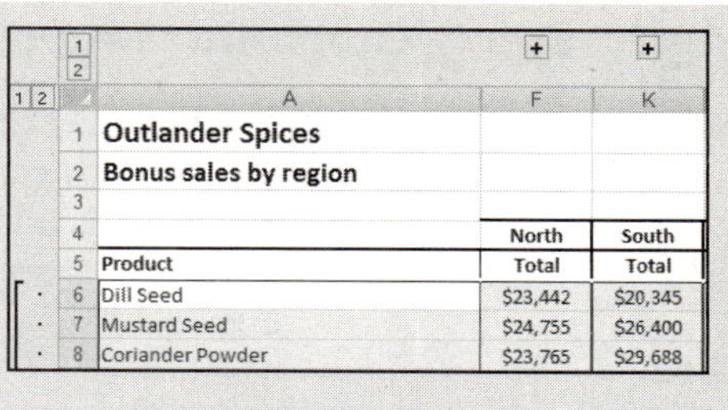

(Click the collapse symbols above columns K, P, U, and Z.) To display only the total sales data for the other regions. Expand symbols will appear above the five visible columns.

6 Click the expand symbol above column F

The quarterly sales data for the North region appears, and there is now a collapse symbol above column F.

7 Click the column-level symbol **2**, as shown

To expand the remaining collapsed column data.

8 Click the row-level symbol **1**

To collapse the row-level data. Detailed data for quarterly sales by product for each region disappears, and only the overall total of quarterly sales for each region is visible.

9 Click the row-level symbol **2**

To expand the row-level data. The worksheet displays the detailed data for the regions.

10 In the Outline group, click as shown

To display a menu.

Choose **Clear Outline**

To clear the outline and return the worksheet to its original state.

11 Update the workbook

Consolidating data

Explanation

You can summarize data from different worksheets by using the data consolidation feature. Data can be consolidated by position or by category. Consolidate by *position* when the related data in the source worksheets is in the same location and order. Consolidate by *category* when data is not in the same location and order. Exhibit 3-3 shows an example of a worksheet with consolidated data.

	A	B	C	D	E
1		Outlander Spices			
2		Bonus sales			
3					
4		Qtr1	Qtr2	Qtr3	Qtr4
9	Anise Seeds	$2,725	$2,114	$2,467	$2,676
14	Asafoetida Powder	$2,674	$2,535	$2,553	$3,208
19	Basil Leaf (Whole)	$29,783	$28,751	$23,478	$33,117
24	Bay Leaf (Whole)	$1,773	$2,780	$2,620	$2,607
29	Caraway Seed (Whole)	$2,263	$3,084	$2,368	$2,112
34	Cardamom Seed (Whole)	$1,277	$2,199	$1,618	$2,619
39	Cardamom Seed (Ground)	$2,489	$2,760	$2,561	$2,804
44	Catnip Leaf	$3,447	$1,466	$1,870	$2,950
49	Celery Seed (Whole)	$24,232	$28,437	$23,697	$18,124
54	Chamomile Flowers	$1,770	$2,591	$2,323	$2,209

Exhibit 3-3: A worksheet with consolidated data

To consolidate data, activate the Data tab. In the Data Tools group, click Consolidate to open the Consolidate dialog box, shown in Exhibit 3-4. The following table explains the options in this dialog box:

Option	Used to...
Function	Choose the aggregate function to consolidate data.
Reference	Specify the cell reference of the source data.
Browse	Navigate among workbooks.
Use labels in	Include row or column headings when you consolidate data by category. When you do not check this option, Excel does not copy category labels from the source area to the destination area.
Create links to source data	Reflect source-data changes in the consolidated data.

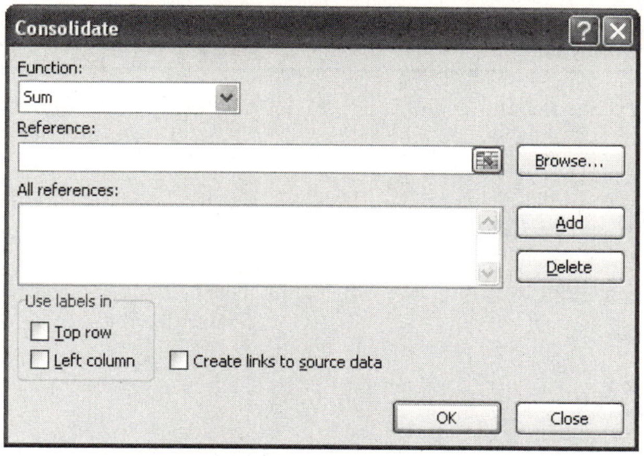

Exhibit 3-4: The Consolidate dialog box

Do it!

A-2: Using the Consolidate command

Here's how	Here's why
1 Open Consolidate	(Leave My Outlining open.) You'll consolidate the sales data for all products in the four regions.
Save the file as **My consolidate**	
2 Activate the Consolidating data worksheet	This is the worksheet where you'll put the consolidated data.
Select A4	
3 Activate the Data tab	If necessary.
4 In the Data Tools group, click **Consolidate**	To open the Consolidate dialog box. In the Function list, Sum is selected by default.
Click	(The Collapse Dialog button is in the Reference box.) To collapse the Consolidate dialog box. The title of the Consolidate dialog box changes to "Consolidate – Reference:", indicating that the Reference box is activated.
5 Activate the North tab	
6 Select A4:E14	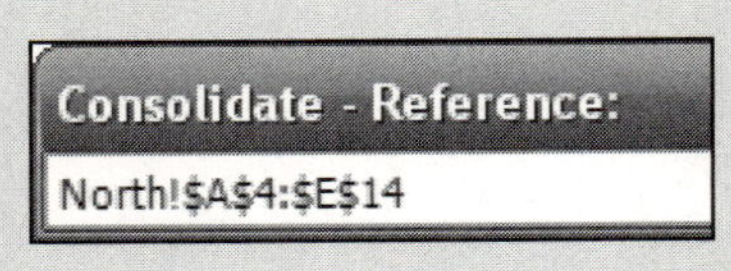 To specify the range, which includes the product and quarter labels. The Consolidate – Reference: box reads North!$A$4:$E$14.
Click	(The Expand Dialog button is in the Consolidate-Reference dialog box.) To expand the Consolidate dialog box.
Click **Add**	To add the range from the North worksheet to the All references list.
7 Activate the South worksheet	To create a reference to the South worksheet. The range A4:E14 is automatically selected. Excel takes the cell or range specified in the last reference as the default for each new reference. The value South!$A$4:$E$14 appears in the Reference box.
Click **Add**	To add the range from the South worksheet to the All references list.

8	Add the references from the East and West worksheets to the All references list	 Activate the worksheet, and click Add in the dialog box.
9	Under Use labels in, check **Top row**	(The Consolidating data worksheet becomes activated.) You'll consolidate data based on the labels in the top row. Excel copies the labels to the destination area when you consolidate data.
	Under Use labels in, check **Left column**	You'll consolidate data based on the labels in the left column.
	Check **Create links to source data**	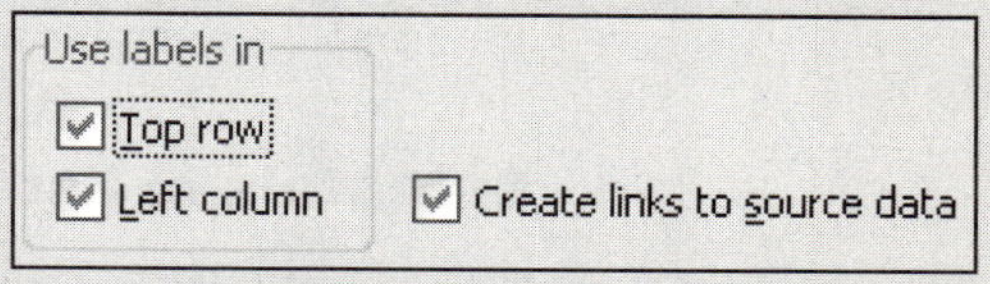 To update the consolidated data automatically when changes are made in the source data.
	Click **OK**	To close the Consolidate dialog box.
10	Deselect the cells	The worksheet shows the total product sales by quarter for the four regions. Outline symbols appear to the left of the worksheet. The worksheet will resemble Exhibit 3-3.
11	Click the row-level expand symbol next to row 9	To display the total sales of anise seeds by region. The total sales figure for each region is listed in the order you specified in the Consolidate dialog box. Excel uses the name of the workbook, "My Consolidate," as the label for each detail row.
	Select C9	 The formula bar shows that the value in C9 is the result of adding C5:C8.
	Select C5	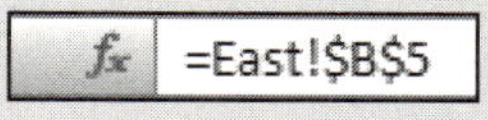 The formula bar shows the formula containing a link to the East worksheet.
12	Update and close the workbook	

Topic B: Creating subtotals

This topic covers the following Microsoft Certified Application Specialist exam objective for Excel 2007.

#	Objective
4.5.2	**Subtotal data** • Add subtotals to grouped data without using the AutoSum button

Summarizing data

Explanation

You can summarize data in a worksheet by calculating subtotals. You can automatically calculate subtotals and grand totals by using functions such as SUM and AVERAGE. You can also use multiple subtotals to summarize the data.

Subtotals in lists

If you want to create automatic subtotals, your list must contain column labels. Moreover, the list must be sorted so that the rows you want to subtotal are grouped together. For example, if you want subtotals for each region, then sort by region first to group the data. You can create subtotals for more than one type of calculation by using various summary functions, such as SUM, MAX, and MIN.

To create subtotals in a list:

1. Sort the list so that the rows you want to subtotal are grouped together.
2. Select any cell in the list and then activate the Data tab.
3. In the Outline group, click Subtotal to open the Subtotal dialog box, shown in Exhibit 3-5.
4. From the “At each change in” list, select the column that contains the groups you want subtotaled.
5. From the Use function list, select the summary function you want to use.
6. In the Add subtotal to list, check the columns for which you want subtotals.
7. Click OK.

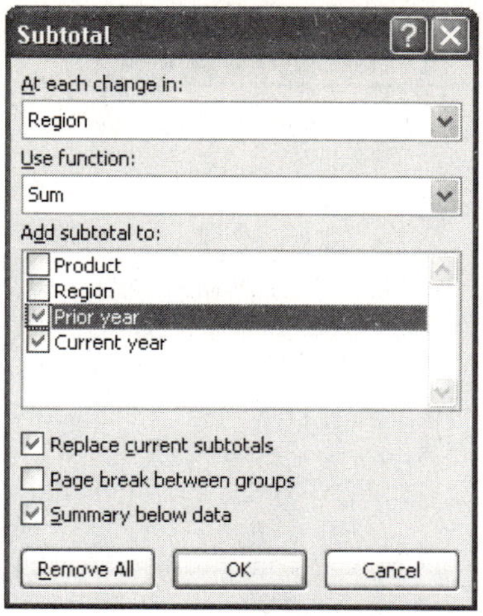

Exhibit 3-5: The Subtotal dialog box

Do it!

B-1: Creating subtotals in a list

Here's how	Here's why
1 In the My outlining workbook, activate the Prior and current sheet	This sheet contains sales totals for two years.
2 Select any cell in the range A4:D52	You'll calculate regional subtotals for the prior and current years' sales.
3 Activate the Data tab	If necessary.
In the Outline group, click **Subtotal**	To open the Subtotal dialog box. The Sum function is selected by default. Notice that Excel automatically selects the sorted list in the worksheet.
4 From the "At each change in" list, select **Region**	To specify the column that contains the groups for which you want subtotals.
Under Add subtotal to, check **Prior year**	As shown in Exhibit 3-5. The rightmost column, Current year, is checked by default. Prior year and Current year are the columns for which you'll create subtotals.
Click **OK**	To close the dialog box. The subtotals for each region appear, along with the grand total for all the regions. Notice that Excel outlines the data.
5 Click the second-level outline button	(see table below) (The numeral 2 to the left of the Column A heading.) To hide the detail. Only the regional subtotals and the grand totals appear.
Expand the sheet to display third-level details	Click the third-level outline button.
6 Update the workbook	

Region	Prior year	Current year
East Total	$447,458	$407,473
North Total	$422,339	$391,866
South Total	$593,807	$596,796
West Total	$605,386	$603,545
Grand Total	$2,068,990	$1,999,680

Multiple subtotal functions

Explanation

You can use more than one subtotal function to provide summary information. First, create a single set of subtotals based on one function. Then add the other functions one at a time. When you add a new function, be sure to clear the Replace current subtotals option in the Subtotal dialog box.

Do it!

B-2: Using multiple subtotal functions

Here's how	Here's why
1 Verify that the Prior and Current sheet is active	You'll add Max and Min subtotals to this list.
2 Select any cell in the list	(If necessary.) You'll use the MAX function to create subtotals for each region.
Open the Subtotal dialog box	(Click Subtotal in the Outline group.) All the options you used earlier are selected.
3 From the Use function list, select **Max**	To display each region's maximum sales for the prior and current years.
Clear **Replace current subtotals**	To retain the existing subtotals.
Click **OK**	The region's maximum sales and overall maximum sales for the Prior year and Current year columns appear.
4 Use the MIN function to add minimum subtotals for the Prior year and Current year columns	Use the Subtotal dialog box.
5 Update and close the workbook	

Unit summary: Outlining and subtotals

Topic A In this topic, you learned how to create an **outline** to summarize data by levels. You also learned how to use the **Consolidate command** to summarize data from several ranges. You learned that you can consolidate by position or by category and that you can create links to the source data.

Topic B In this topic, you learned how to create **subtotals** that summarize worksheet data. You used the Subtotal dialog box to create various summary formulas.

Independent practice activity

In this activity, you'll outline a sheet with a large amount of data to make it more manageable, and create subtotals.

1. Open Outlining practice. (Ensure that the Outlining worksheet is active.)
2. Save the workbook as **My outlining practice**.
3. Create an automatic outline for the data in the Outlining worksheet.
4. Collapse columns and rows to display only summary information.
5. Consolidate the data from the East and West worksheets, beginning in A4 in the Consolidate worksheet. (*Hint:* Use A4:E9 as the range in both sheets, use row and column labels, and link to the source data.)
6. Activate the Subtotals worksheet.
7. Create subtotals for each product for the Prior year and Current year columns by using the SUM, AVERAGE, and MAX functions. Do not replace the current subtotals.
8. Update and close the workbook.

Review questions

1. How does outlining help you work with large amounts of data?

2. When should you consolidate by position, and when should you consolidate by category?

3. How do you make the Consolidate command summarize data from multiple worksheets even if the row headings aren't in the same position in each sheet?

4. If you want to create automatic subtotals, what must your list contain?

Unit 4

Cell and range names

Unit time: 55 minutes

Complete this unit, and you'll know how to:

A Use names to make your formulas easier to understand.

B Use the Name Manager, and define 3-D names, which span multiple worksheets.

Topic A: Creating and using names

This topic covers the following Microsoft Certified Application Specialist exam objectives for Excel 2007.

#	Objective
3.1.3	**Manage named ranges** • Select and name a range of cells
3.1.4	**Use named ranges in formulas** • Using sales figures named in three ranges, create formulas for sales figures that summarize the sales figures for three teams

Naming cells

Explanation

A name is a meaningful description that you assign to a cell or range. After a name has been assigned, you can use it in formulas in place of cell references, making your formulas easier to understand. For example, in the formula `=SUM(Qtr1)`, Qtr1 is the name assigned to the range of cells containing Quarter 1 data.

Defining names for cells or ranges

Names must begin with a letter or an underscore, cannot include spaces, and cannot match a cell address. For example, Q_1 is a valid name, but Q 1 is not (because of the space), and Q1 is not (because it's a cell address).

To define a name:

1. Select the cell or range that you want to name.
2. Enter the name in the Name box at the left edge of the formula bar.

You can select a named range by choosing it from the Name list to the right of the Name box.

Do it!

A-1: Naming and selecting ranges

Here's how	Here's why
1 Open Names	(From the current unit folder.) You'll define names to represent ranges in this workbook. You'll also use these names in formulas.
2 Save the workbook as **My names**	In the current unit folder.
Verify that the Team sales worksheet is active	
3 Select A5:D5	You'll name this range Wilcox.
Edit the Name box to read **Wilcox**	 The Name box is located at the left edge of the formula bar.
Press ENTER	
4 Select A14:D14	
Name the range **Pincus**	Click in the Name box, type Pincus, and press Enter.
Name A23:D23 **Springer**	
5 From the Name list, select **Pincus**, as indicated	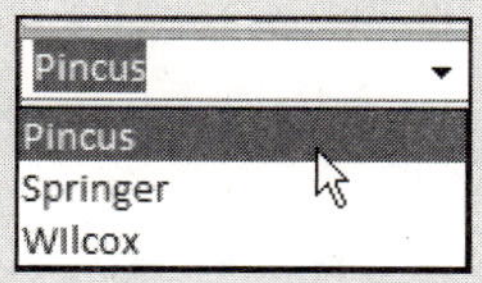 (Display the name list by clicking the arrow to the right of the Name box.) Cells A14:D14, the cells represented by the name Pincus, are selected.
6 Update the workbook	

Using a named range as a reference in a formula

Explanation

One of the primary reasons to name a range is so you can use the name in a formula to make it easier to understand. For example, =SUM (Qtr1_Sales) is more readily identifiable than =SUM (B3:B15). After a cell or range has been named, you can substitute the name for the cell address or range address in a formula.

To use a name in a formula, you can do either of the following:

- In the Defined Names group on the Formulas tab, click Use in Formula; then select the name you want to use in the formula.
- Begin typing the name in the formula; then select an item from the AutoComplete list that appears. You can use arrow keys to select the item and then press Tab to enter it in the formula.

Do it!

A-2: Using names in formulas

Here's how	Here's why
1 Activate the Formulas tab	
Select B31	You'll use the name Wilcox instead of the range address to sum the quarterly sales values for the Wilcox team.
2 Type **=SUM(**	To begin the SUM function. You'll select the named range from a list.
3 In the Defined Names group, click **Use in Formula**	To open a list of named cells and ranges.
Select **Wilcox**	To add the name to the formula you began.
4 Press ENTER	To complete the formula.
5 Select B31	
Observe the formula	The formula =SUM(Wilcox) is easier to understand than one that contains a range address.
6 Select B32	(If necessary.) You'll use AutoComplete to enter the name.
Type **=SUM(P**	A list of possible names and functions appears.
In the list, double-click **Pincus**	To add it to the formula.
Press ENTER	To complete the formula.
7 In B33, enter a formula that sums the bonus sales of the Springer team	Use any method you like.
8 Update the workbook	

The Create from Selection command

Explanation

It can be tedious to create named ranges by manually entering each name. Instead, you can use column and row labels as names for the cells they represent. To create names by using existing labels:

1. Select the range or ranges you want to name, including the row or column labels. (The cells containing the row or column labels won't be included in the named range. They are selected to provide the appropriate labels.)
2. In the Defined Names group on the Formulas tab, click Create from Selection to open the Create Names from Selection dialog box, shown in Exhibit 4-1.
3. Specify the locations of the labels in the selected range.
4. Click OK.

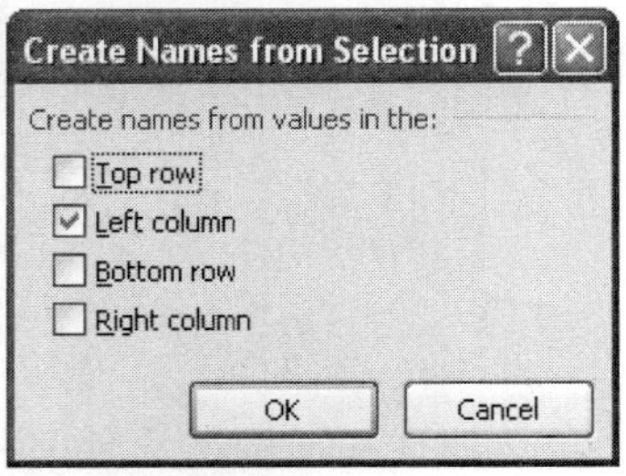

Exhibit 4-1: The Create Names from Selection dialog box

Do it!

A-3: Using the Create from Selection command

Here's how	Here's why
1 Activate the East sheet	
Select A5:E9	By using the labels in the range A5:A9, you'll name the respective rows in the range B5:E9. For example, B5:E5 will use the label "Anise Seeds."
2 In the Defined Names group, click **Create from Selection**	To open the Create Names from Selection dialog box, shown in Exhibit 4-1. "Left column" is checked because the selected range contains labels in the left column.
Click **OK**	To close the dialog box, creating a name for each row in the range B5:E9.
3 Select B5:E5	The name of the selected range appears as Anise_Seeds. Excel adds an underscore to the label to make the name conform to the naming requirements.
4 Observe the names of the ranges B6:E6, B7:E7, B8:E8, and B9:E9	Select a range and observe the Name box.
5 Activate the West sheet	You'll name ranges in this sheet.
6 Name cells B4:F9 by using the top row labels	(Select B4:F9 and click Create from Selection to open the Create Names from Selection dialog box. Then, click OK.) If you don't select the top-row labels (B4:F4), names will not be created.
Verify that names have been created	(Click the Name box's down-arrow.) You should see the names Qtr_1, Qtr_2, Qtr_3, Qtr_4, and Total in the list.
7 Update the workbook	

The Apply Names command

Explanation

You might work with spreadsheets in which formulas have already been entered with cell references rather than named ranges. If you want to replace those references in formulas, you can use the Apply Names command.

Apply Names is also useful—particularly for copying formulas—if you enter formulas after creating names. If you copy and paste, or AutoFill, a formula that uses a named range, Excel treats that name as an absolute reference (as it would a cell reference like $B$10). For example, when you copy =SUM(Q1_sales) to the column to its right, the formula will still be =SUM(Q1_sales), not = SUM(Q2_sales) as you might expect.

In this instance, you can create the formula without using the named range, and then use the Apply Names command to replace the cell reference in each autofilled cell with its equivalent name.

To apply names:

1. Select cells that contain formulas with cell references that you want to replace with names.
2. In the Defined Names group on the Formulas tab, click the Define Name drop-down arrow and choose Apply Names. The Apply Names dialog box, shown in Exhibit 4-2, will open.
3. From the Apply names list, select the names you want to apply. You need only click to add to the selection (unlike with many lists, in which you need to Shift+click or Ctrl+click).
4. Click OK.

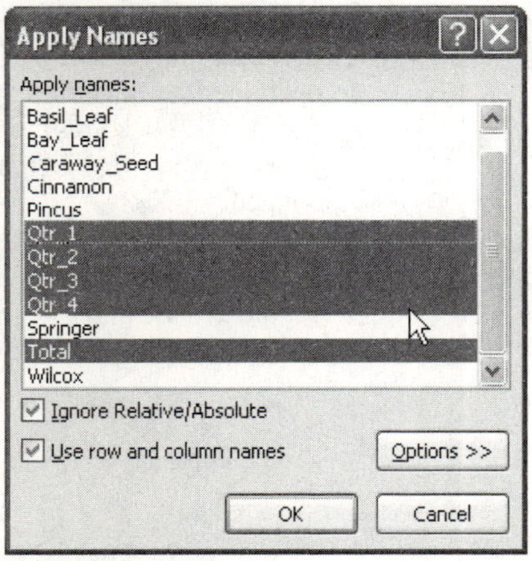

Exhibit 4-2: The Apply Names dialog box

Do it!

A-4: Applying names to existing formulas

Here's how	Here's why
1 Select B10	
2 Observe the formula bar	
	Because this formula was created before you defined names for the Qtr columns, the argument in the formula is the range B5:B9, not Qtr_1.
Observe the formulas for C10, D10, E10, and F10	These SUM formulas also use cell references, not names. You'll apply the names you created to these formulas.
Select B10:F10	
3 In the Defined Names group, click the down-arrow beside Define Name and choose **Apply Names...**	To open the Apply Names dialog box, shown in Exhibit 4-2.
Verify that the Qtr and Total names are selected, as shown	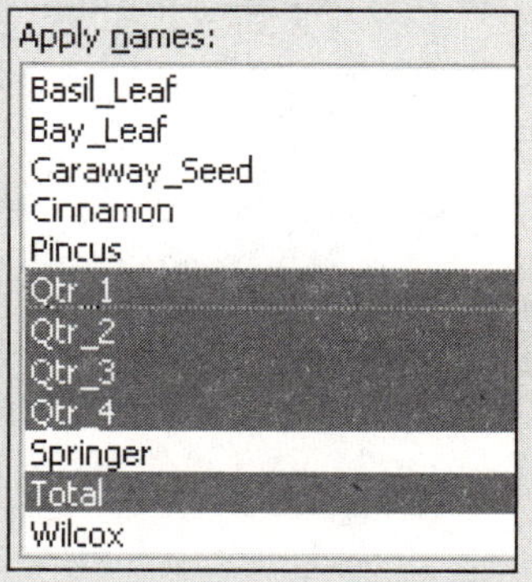
Click **OK**	To close the dialog box and apply these names.
4 Select B10	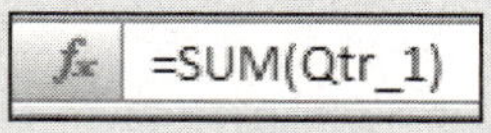
	In the formula bar, the range has been replaced by the name Qtr_1.
Observe the formulas for C10, D10, E10, and F10	The SUM formulas use names instead of cell references.
	Another reason to apply names is that AutoFill doesn't work as you'd likely intend if you use it starting with a named range.
5 Activate the East sheet	You'll total the Anise_Seeds range.

6	Select F5	
	Activate the Home tab	
	In the Editing group, click **Σ**	The AutoSum button automatically inserts the name rather than the range address.
	Press ENTER	The formula refers to the name Anise_Seeds
7	Select F5; then drag its AutoFill handle down to fill F6:F10	The value in F5 repeats, because each formula sums the Anise_Seeds range.
	On the Quick Access toolbar, click [Undo] twice	To delete the values in each of the Total column cells.
8	Select B5:F10	
	In the Editing group, click **Σ**	To autosum the quarterly sales.
	Select F5 and observe the formula	When applied to a range, the AutoSum button inserts cell references, not names, in each cell.
9	Activate the Formulas tab	
	Select F5:F10	You'll replace the cell references with names.
10	Click the arrow next to Define Name and choose **Apply Names...**	
	Select names as shown	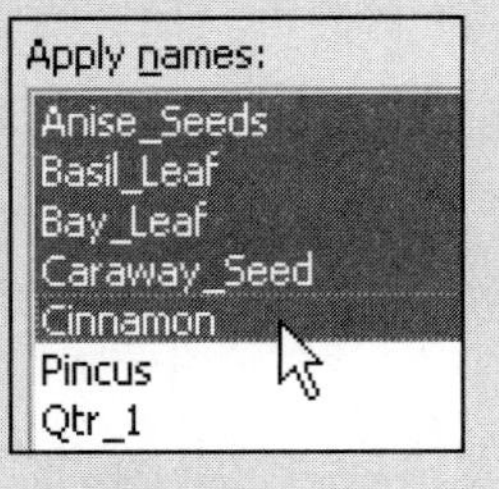 Click each name to select it.
	Click **OK**	To close the dialog box and apply the names.
	Check each formula in F5:F9	The named ranges appear instead of the cell references.
11	Update the workbook	

Topic B: Managing names

This topic covers the following Microsoft Certified Application Specialist exam objective for Excel 2007.

#	Objective
3.1.3	**Manage named ranges** • Modify a named range by adding a column • Delete a named range

Names in multiple worksheets

Explanation

When you create names in a workbook with multiple worksheets, you might need to manage the names to avoid reference problems. For example, if you create the same name in multiple sheets, it might be unclear which range to go to or use in a formula. You can use the Name Manager dialog box and 3-D names to handle named ranges in multiple sheets.

The Name Manager

When you've created several names in a workbook, you might find the Name Manager dialog box, shown in Exhibit 4-3, useful for viewing and editing their properties. You can also use it to define new names and to delete multiple names quickly. To open this dialog box, click Name Manager in the Defined Names group on the Formulas tab.

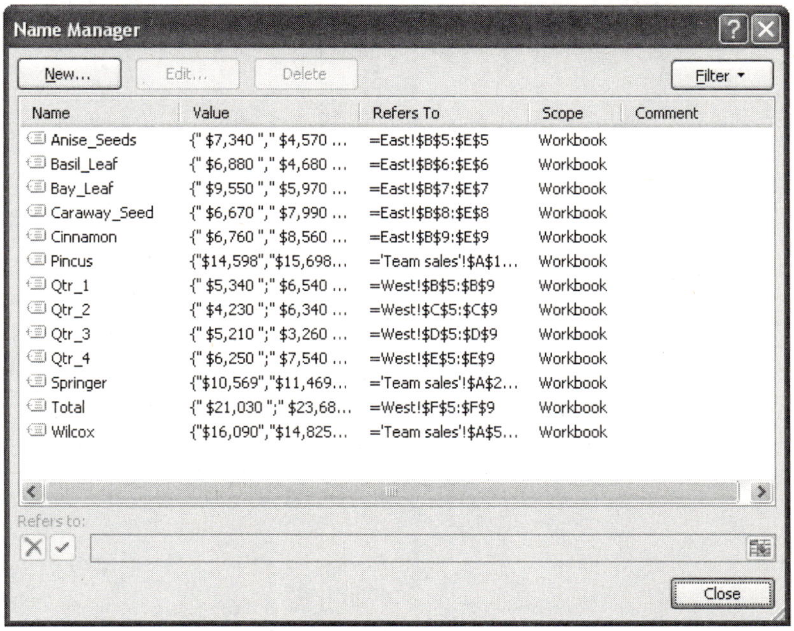

Exhibit 4-3: The Name Manager dialog box

Using the Name Manager to change and delete names

To use the Name Manager to modify a named range, select the name in the list and click Edit. The Edit Name dialog box opens, allowing you to edit the name itself, add comments, or change the cell references. When you are finished making changes, click OK.

When you want to delete a named range, select the name in the Name Manager and click Delete. A message box will appear, asking you to confirm the deletion.

Do it!

B-1: Modifying and deleting named ranges

Here's how	Here's why
1 Activate the Team sales worksheet	You'll modify the defined names to include the Inventory costs column
2 On the Formulas tab, in the Defined Names group, click **Name Manager**	To open the Name Manager dialog box. It contains a list of all names in the workbook, as well as their values and cell references.
3 In the Name list, select **Wilcox**	When a name is selected in the list, the Edit and Delete buttons become available.
Click **Edit**	To open the Edit Name dialog box. You'll change the cell references in the name.
4 Click 	(The Collapse Dialog button is to the right of the Refers to box.) To collapse the dialog box and show only the cells the name currently references. The range A5:D5 is selected in the worksheet.
Select A5:E5	To change the cell references to include the new column. The Edit Name – Refers to: box now includes the new range.
Click 	To expand the dialog box.
5 Click **OK**	To close the Edit Name dialog box and apply the new range to the name.
Click **Close**	To close the Name Manager.
6 Scroll down to B31	The value has changed from $66,892 to $53,912.
7 Open the Name Manager	In the Defined Names group, click Name Manager.
In the Name list, select **Wilcox**	
8 Click **Delete**	A message box appears, asking you to confirm the deletion.
Click **OK**	To delete the name Wilcox.
9 Click **Close**	To close the Name Manager. Notice that an error now appears in B31 because it references a name that no longer exists.
Update the workbook	

3-D names

Explanation

You can define names that refer to the same cell or range in multiple worksheets. These names are called *3-D names*. A 3-D name is typically useful in formulas that compile results from multiple sheets, such as one to total sales across multiple regions or time periods. Exhibit 4-4 shows a 3-D name that includes the cell F10 in all of the spreadsheets from the East sheet through the West sheet.

To create a 3-D name:

1. In the Name Manager dialog box, click New.
2. Delete the value in the Refers to box.
3. Click a sheet tab to establish the starting sheet in the range.
4. Hold Shift and click another sheet to determine the ending sheet.
5. Click a cell to insert its address in the reference.
6. Click OK.

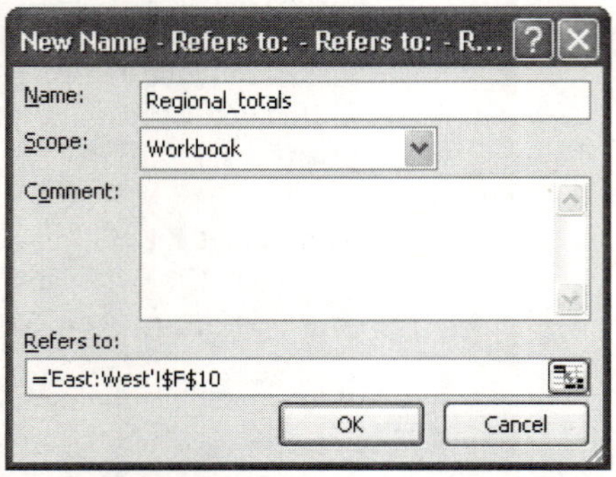

Exhibit 4-4: The New Name dialog box with a 3-D name defined

Do it!

B-2: Defining and applying 3-D names

Here's how	Here's why
1 Open the Name Manager	
2 Click **New**	To open the New Name dialog box. You'll create a name for the combination of the Total cells in both regions.
In the Name box, enter **Regional_totals**	You'll define a 3-D name that refers to B10 across the worksheet range East:West.
In the Refers to box, delete the reference	If necessary.
3 Click	To collapse the New Name dialog box so it covers fewer cells in the workbook.
Click the **East** sheet tab	To specify the first worksheet to be referenced.
While holding SHIFT, click the **West** sheet tab	To specify the last worksheet to be referenced in the range East:West.
Select F10	='East:West'!$F$10 To specify the cell to be referenced across the specified worksheet range.
Click	(The Expand Dialog button is to the right of the Refers to box.) To expand the New Name dialog box.
4 Click **OK**	To add Regional_totals to the names list. This name will not appear in the Name box because it is a 3-D range, which refers to multiple worksheets.
Click **Close**	To close the Name Manager dialog box.
5 Activate the Total sales sheet	(If necessary.) The formula that will refer to the Regional_totals range should go in F10.
6 Select F10	
7 Type **=SUM(Regional_totals)**	
8 Press ENTER	The value of $241,400 is the sum of cells F10 in the East and West sheets.
9 Update and close the workbook	

Unit summary: Cell and range names

Topic A In this topic, you learned how to define **names** and select **named ranges**. You learned how to use names in functions to make them more readable, and how to **create names from selections** based on column and row labels. You also learned how to use the **Apply Names** command to replace the cell references in formulas with names.

Topic B In this topic, you learned about using the **Name Manager** to manage names. You learned how to edit a named range and how to delete a name. You also learned how to create **3-D names**, which span multiple worksheets.

Independent practice activity

In this activity, you'll specify names for ranges within individual sheets and across multiple sheets.

1 Open Names practice.

2 Save the workbook as **My names practice**.

3 On the Performance worksheet, define names to refer to the ranges B5:B20 and C5:C20. (*Hint:* Use the Create From Selection command, and include the column title in the selection.)

4 Apply the new names to the range B5:D21. Observe how names are used in the formulas in column D.

5 Define a 3-D name called **Regional_totals** that refers to F10 in the North and South sheets.

6 Use the name in a SUM formula in F10 in the Total sales sheet.

7 Delete the name **Regional_totals**.

8 Update and close the workbook.

Review questions

1 What is a name?

2 Names must begin with a letter or an underscore and can include spaces. True or false?

3 What command can you use to create several names simultaneously?

4 What is the advantage of using a named cell or range in a formula?

5 By default, a cell name can be referenced from any sheet in a workbook. True or false?

6 How can you create a 3-D name to span multiple worksheets?

Unit 5
Lists and tables

Unit time: 55 minutes

Complete this unit, and you'll know how to:

A Use lists to organize data logically.

B Sort lists by the contents of their columns, and filter lists to show only those rows that meet certain criteria.

C Use the Custom AutoFilter and Advanced Filter dialog boxes to filter lists based on complex criteria.

D Create and format tables, and apply structured referencing to include their column names in formulas.

Topic A: Examining lists

Explanation

You can create lists in your worksheets to organize data in a concise and logical format. A *list* is a series of rows containing related data.

List structure

A list is made up of records, fields, and field names. *Records* are simply the rows of data in a list. *Fields* are the columns of data in a list. *Field names* are the column headings, which appear in the first row of the list. A sample Excel list is shown in Exhibit 5-1.

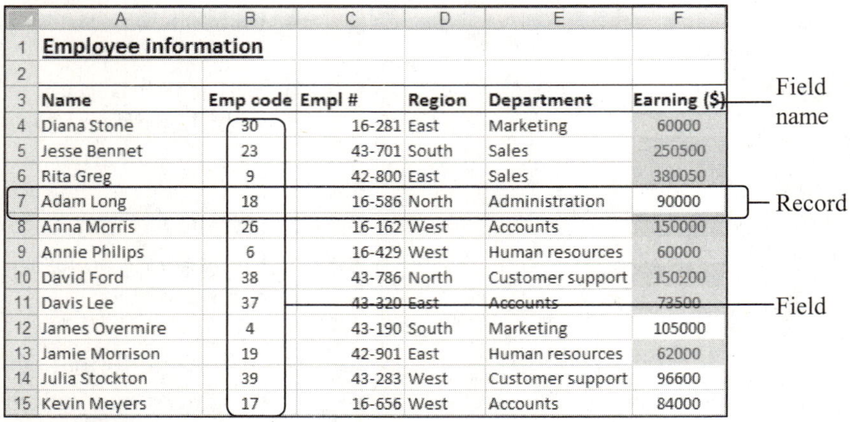

	A	B	C	D	E	F
1	Employee information					
2						
3	Name	Emp code	Empl #	Region	Department	Earning ($)
4	Diana Stone	30	16-281	East	Marketing	60000
5	Jesse Bennet	23	43-701	South	Sales	250500
6	Rita Greg	9	42-800	East	Sales	380050
7	Adam Long	18	16-586	North	Administration	90000
8	Anna Morris	26	16-162	West	Accounts	150000
9	Annie Philips	6	16-429	West	Human resources	60000
10	David Ford	38	43-786	North	Customer support	150200
11	Davis Lee	37	43-320	East	Accounts	73500
12	James Overmire	4	43-190	South	Marketing	105000
13	Jamie Morrison	19	42-901	East	Human resources	62000
14	Julia Stockton	39	43-283	West	Customer support	96600
15	Kevin Meyers	17	16-656	West	Accounts	84000

Exhibit 5-1: The structure of a list

Do it!

A-1: Examining the structure of a list

Here's how	Here's why
1 Open Employee information	(From the current unit folder.) You'll examine the structure of the Employee information list.
Save the workbook as **My employee information**	In the current unit folder.
2 Observe A3:F3	The column headings in this range are the field names for this list.
3 Observe A5:F5	This row represents one record. In this list, each record contains all the related information for an individual employee.
4 Observe A4:F43	Each cell represents a field value for a specific record.

Topic B: Sorting and filtering lists

This topic covers the following Microsoft Certified Application Specialist exam objectives for Excel 2007.

#	Objective
4.6.1	**Sort data by using single or multiple criteria**
4.6.3	**Filter and sort data by using conditional formatting**
4.6.4	**Filter and sort data by using cell attributes**

Organizing data

Explanation

Sorting refers to organizing the data in a list in ascending or descending order by the contents of one or more columns in the list. *Filtering* refers to displaying only the information that meets specific criteria.

Sorting lists

To sort a list, select any cell in the column by which you want to sort. Activate the Data tab. In the Sort & Filter group, click the Sort Ascending button or the Sort Descending button. This will sort the entire list, including all records, not just the column containing the selected cell.

Sorting lists based on two or more columns

You can also sort a list based on data in two or more columns. For example, you can sort employee information by region and department, as shown in Exhibit 5-2. In this case, all the employees in a single region are grouped together and then sorted by department.

	A	B	C	D	E	F
1	**Employee information**					
2						
3	**Name**	**Emp code**	**Empl #**	**Region**	**Department**	**Earning ($)**
4	Melissa James	7	16-129	East	Accounts	87000
5	Davis Lee	37	43-320	East	Accounts	73500
6	Wendy Alto	34	43-730	East	Administration	105000
7	Sonia McCormick	40	16-192	East	Administration	78000
8	Roger Williams	5	43-763	East	Customer support	90000
9	Malcolm Pingault	1	16-891	East	Human resources	72000
10	Paul Anderson	11	43-133	East	Human resources	180000
11	Jamie Morrison	19	42-901	East	Human resources	62000
12	Diana Stone	30	16-281	East	Marketing	60000
13	Sandy Stewart	33	43-129	East	Marketing	65000
14	Rita Greg	9	42-800	East	Sales	380050
15	Kendra James	16	16-111	East	Sales	144000
16	Sandra Lawrence	15	43-487	North	Accounts	100000
17	Mary Smith	8	43-314	North	Administration	104000

Exhibit 5-2: The Employee information list sorted by Region and Department

To sort a list based on two or more columns:

1. Select any cell in the list.
2. Activate the Data tab.
3. In the Sort & Filter group, click Sort to open the Sort dialog box, shown in Exhibit 5-3.
4. From the Sort by list, select the heading of the column by which you want to sort the list. Then select a sorting order. All records will be sorted first based on the column and the sorting order you selected.
5. If necessary, click Add Level to add another sort level. From the Then by list, select the next column by which you want to sort, and select the sort order.
6. Click OK.

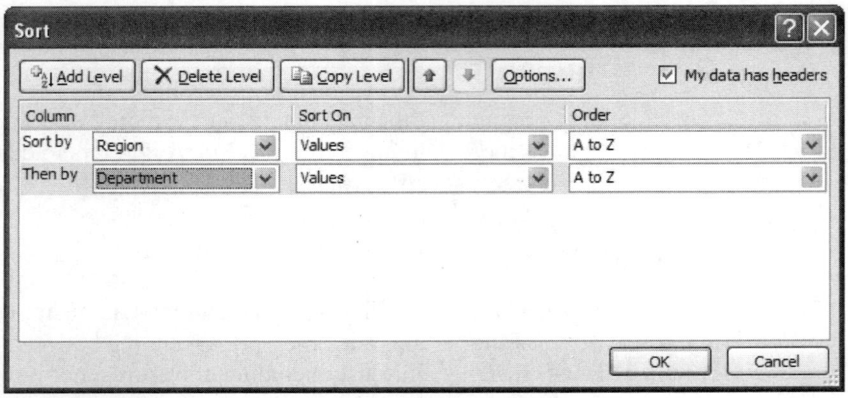

Exhibit 5-3: The Sort dialog box, with a second sort level added

Do it!

B-1: Sorting a list

Here's how	Here's why
1 Select B4	You'll sort the rows of employee information by the contents of this column, Emp code, in ascending order. You can select any cell in the column you want to sort by.
Activate the Data tab	
2 In the Sort & Filter group, click 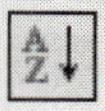	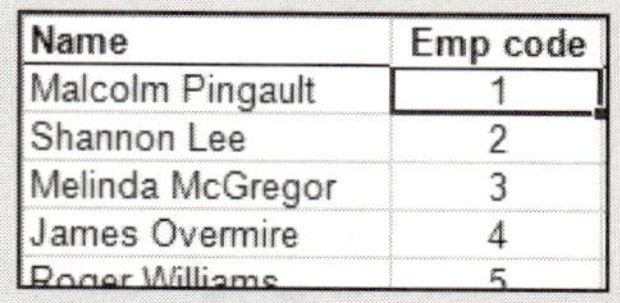 (The Sort Smallest to Largest button.) The rows are now organized in ascending order by employee code.
3 Select any cell in the list	(If necessary.) You'll sort the data by multiple fields.
4 Click **Sort**	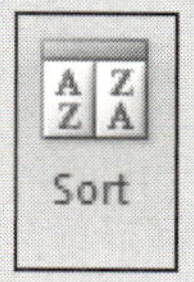 (The Sort button is in the Sort & Filter group.) To open the Sort dialog box.
Under Column, from the Sort by list, select **Region**	To specify that the list be sorted first by region.
Under Sort on, verify that Values is selected	To sort by the contents of the cells.
Under Order, select **A to Z**	(If necessary.) The list will be sorted by region in ascending (alphabetical) order.
5 Click **Add Level**	To add a second criterion to this sort.
6 Under Column, from the Then by list, select **Department**	When rows have the same value in the Region column, they will be sorted by department. The default order is Ascending, as shown in Exhibit 5-3.
Click **OK**	To display the sorted list in the worksheet. All the employees in a region are now grouped together, beginning with the East region. For each region, the department names are sorted in ascending alphabetical order, as shown in Exhibit 5-2.
7 Update the workbook	

Filtering lists

Explanation

You can *filter* a list when you want to display only those rows of information that meet specific criteria. To help you do this, Excel provides the AutoFilter feature. Here's how it works:

1. Select any cell in the list.
2. Activate the Data tab.
3. In the Sort & Filter group, click Filter to display the AutoFilter arrows next to each column heading.
4. From the list for the column by which you want to filter, select a criterion, as shown in Exhibit 5-4.
5. Click OK.

To clear the filter and show the entire list, click Filter again.

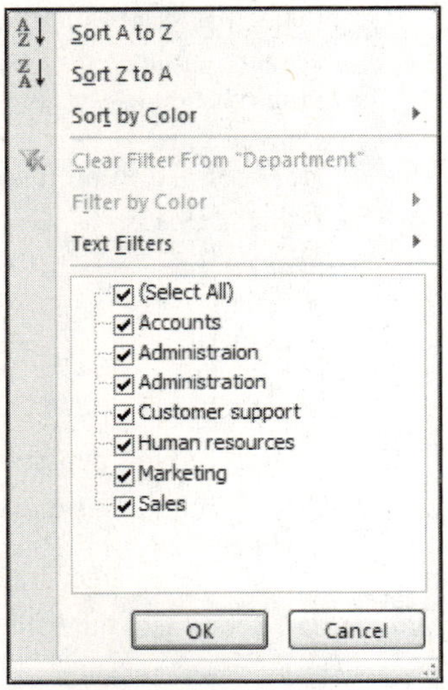

Exhibit 5-4: The AutoFilter list

Do it!

B-2: Filtering a list by using AutoFilter

Here's how	Here's why
1 Select any cell in the list	If necessary.
2 Activate the Data tab	If necessary.
3 Click **Filter**	In the Sort & Filter group.
Observe the column headings	 The AutoFilter arrows appear to the right of all of the column headings.
4 Click the AutoFilter arrow next to Department	To display a list of sorting and filtering criteria, as shown in Exhibit 5-4.
5 Clear **Select All**	To clear the department selections.
Check **Accounts**	To display only the records of employees in the Accounts department. All other records will be hidden.
Click **OK**	To filter the list.
6 From the Region list, select only **West**	To display only the records of those employees in the Accounts department who work in the West region.
7 Click the AutoFilter arrow next to Department and choose **Clear Filter from "Department"**	The list is no longer filtered by department.
Clear the Region filter	(Click the AutoFilter arrow and choose Clear Filter from "Region".) The list is no longer filtered by region.
8 Update the workbook	

Using other criteria to sort and filter data

Explanation

You can use a variety of criteria to sort and filter lists. For example, you can use a cell color or font color as your sorting or filtering criterion. You can also select a cell and sort your list based on that cell's attributes, such as its formatting or its value.

To sort and filter data based on cell color or font color, click the arrow next to the column heading that contains the values you want to sort or filter. From the menu, choose Sort by Color or Filter by Color, and select the fill or font color by which you want to sort or filter.

To sort and filter based on a cell's attributes, right-click the selected cell. From the shortcut menu, choose the option you want to sort or filter by.

Do it!

B-3: Using cell color and attributes to sort and filter data

Here's how	Here's why
1 Observe the Earning column	The values in this column have been conditionally formatted to highlight the top 10 earning values in light red, and the bottom 10 values in light green.
Display the sort-and-filter menu for the Earning column	(Click the arrow on the column header.) You'll sort the column based on one of the conditional formats.
2 Choose **Sort by Color**	To display a submenu.
Click as shown	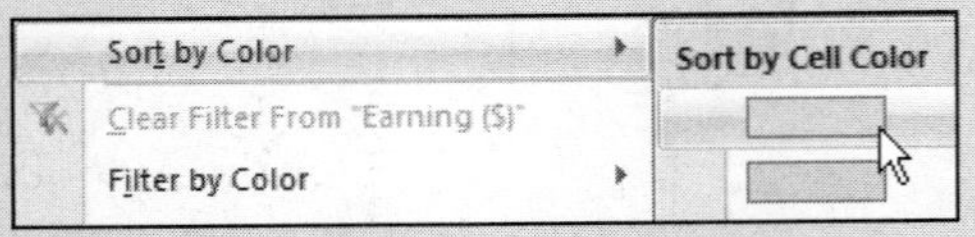 To sort by the indicated fill color. The list is sorted with the bottom ten earning values now at the top of the list.
3 Select F21	You'll filter the list by the value in this cell.
Right-click the cell	To display a shortcut menu.
4 Choose **Filter**, **Filter by Selected Cell's Value**	To find all the column values that match the value in the selected cell. Two cells are in the list.
5 Clear the filter	
Update the workbook	

Topic C: Advanced filtering

This topic covers the following Microsoft Certified Application Specialist exam objective for Excel 2007.

#	Objective
4.6.2	**Filter data by using AutoFilter** • Filter data by using Custom AutoFilter

Tools for filtering by multiple criteria

Explanation

You can filter a list based on two or more criteria by using Excel's advanced filtering features. For example, you can display the records of all employees whose department is either Marketing or Sales. Excel provides two tools for specifying multiple filter criteria:

- Custom AutoFilter
- Advanced Filter

Custom AutoFilter

Use the Custom AutoFilter dialog box to specify multiple criteria for the same column heading, as shown in Exhibit 5-5.

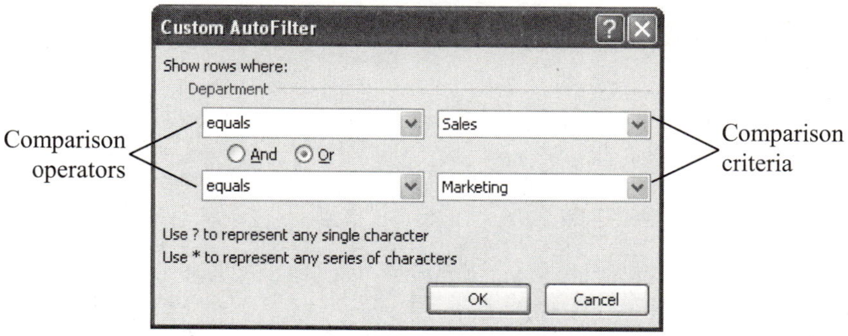

Exhibit 5-5: The Custom AutoFilter dialog box

In Exhibit 5-5, Department is the column on which the data will be filtered. The first criterion states that the department must be Sales; the second criterion states that the department must be Marketing. The two criteria are joined by the Or operator, meaning that rows will be included in the filtered list if they meet *either* criterion. When you use the And operator, the rows must meet *both* criteria. The criteria in Exhibit 5-5 would yield a list of all employees who work in either the Sales or Marketing departments.

To filter a list by using the Custom AutoFilter dialog box:

1. Turn on AutoFilter for the list.
2. Display the drop-down menu for the column for which you want to create criteria. Then choose Text Filters, Custom Filter to open the Custom AutoFilter dialog box.
3. Select the first comparison operator and its associated criterion.
4. Select And or Or. By selecting And, you'll decrease the number of rows that meet the criteria. By selecting Or, you'll increase the number of matching rows.
5. Select the second comparison operator and its associated criterion.
6. Click OK.

Do it!

C-1: Using Custom AutoFilter criteria

Here's how	Here's why
1 Click the AutoFilter arrow next to Department	To display the sorting and filtering criteria. You'll display the records of those employees who belong to either the Sales department or the Marketing department.
2 Choose **Text Filters, Custom Filter...**	To open the Custom AutoFilter dialog box. In the upper-left list, the first comparison operator, equals, is selected.
From the upper-right list, select **Sales**	 To specify the first comparison criterion.
Select **Or**	This tells Excel to display all records that match either of the two comparison criteria.
3 From the lower-left list, select **equals**	To specify the second comparison operator.
From the lower-right list, select **Marketing**	To specify the second comparison criterion. The Custom AutoFilter dialog box now resembles Exhibit 5-5.
Click **OK**	The worksheet displays records of employees who work in either the Sales department or the Marketing department.
4 In the Sort & Filter group, click **Clear**	The list is no longer filtered by these two criteria. AutoFilter remains active.

Creating a criteria range

Explanation

You can filter records based on two or more column headings by using multiple criteria. For example, you can filter a list to display the records of all East region employees whose salaries are greater than $100,000 and all West region employees whose salaries are greater than or equal to $80,000. A criteria range filters data based on complex criteria.

A *criteria range* is a cell range containing a set of search conditions. It consists of one row of criteria labels and at least one row that defines the search conditions. Each criterion label must be the name of a column for which you want to specify a criterion. The Advanced Filter dialog box filters a list according to a criteria range.

The following table lists the comparison operators that can be used in a criteria range:

Operator	Meaning
=	Equal to
>	Greater than
<	Less than
>=	Greater than or equal to
<=	Less than or equal to
<>	Not equal to

To create a criteria range by using the Advanced Filter dialog box:

1. Enter at least one criterion label in a cell that is *not* adjacent to the range containing the list. The criterion label must be exactly the same as the column heading in the list.
2. Below the cell that contains the criterion label, enter a comparison criterion.
3. Activate the Data tab.
4. In the Sort & Filter group, click Advanced to open the Advanced Filter dialog box, shown in Exhibit 5-6.
5. In the List range box, enter the range you want to filter. The range must include the associated column headings.
6. In the Criteria range box, enter the range that contains your criteria.
7. Click OK.

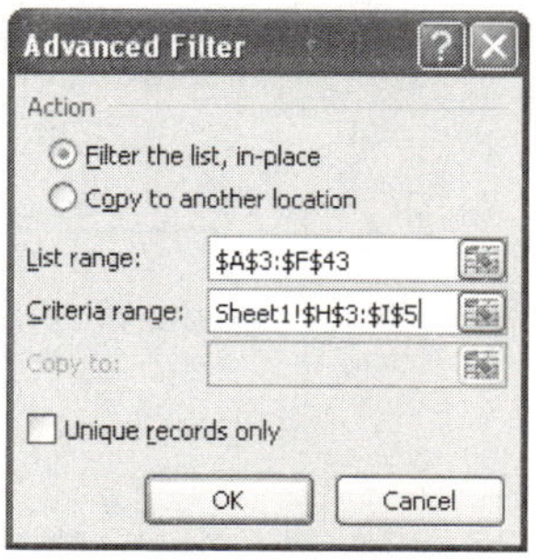

Exhibit 5-6: The Advanced Filter dialog box, filtering the list in place

Do it!

C-2: Using the Advanced Filter dialog box

Here's how	Here's why
1 In H3, type **Region**	To specify the first criterion label. Ensure that it matches the column heading in the list exactly. Copying and pasting the column headings is a good way to ensure that the labels are identical to those in the list.
In I3, enter **Earning ($)**	To specify the second criterion label. Be sure to include the space between Earning and ($). Or, copy and paste the heading from F3.
2 In H4, enter **East**	To specify East as the first comparison criterion.
In I4, enter **>100000**	To complete the first row of criteria. These criteria will display only those values in the East region with earnings greater than $100,000.
3 In H5, enter **West**	To specify West as the criterion.
In I5, enter **>=80000**	The second row of the criteria range will display values in the West region with earnings greater than or equal to $80,000. Adding rows to a criteria range amounts to using an Or operator, so rows will be included if they meet either of these conditions.
4 Select any cell in the original list	(In the range A4:F43.) You'll enter the entire list range automatically when you choose the Advanced Filter command.
In the Sort & Filter group, click **Advanced**	To open the Advanced Filter dialog box. "Filter the list, in-place" is selected by default. This means that the filtered list will be displayed in the same worksheet. The entire list appears selected in the worksheet.
5 Beside the Criteria range box, click	 (The Collapse Dialog button.) The Advanced Filter – Criteria range: dialog box appears.
Select H3:I5	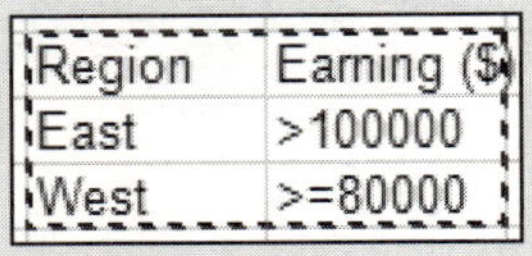 To enter the criteria range.

6 Click [Expand Dialog button]	(The Expand Dialog button is in the Advanced Filter – Criteria range: dialog box.) To expand the dialog box, as shown in Exhibit 5-6.
Click **OK**	The list now displays the records of the four employees in the East region whose salaries are greater than $100,000, as well as the nine employees in the West region whose salaries are greater than or equal to $80,000.
7 Display the unfiltered list	Click Clear in the Sort & Filter group.
8 Update the workbook	

Copying filtered results to another location

Explanation

In the examples you've seen so far, rows are filtered out of the list so that all you can see are the remaining rows. You can also choose to keep the original list intact and place a copy of the filtered list somewhere else in the same worksheet or in another worksheet in the workbook. To do so, select the "Copy to another location" option in the Advanced Filter dialog box, and then specify a starting cell for the copied list, as shown in Exhibit 5-7.

Exhibit 5-7: The Advanced Filter dialog box, copying the filtered list to another location

Do it!

C-3: Copying filtered results to another range

Here's how	Here's why
1 Select a cell in the Name list	If necessary.
2 Open the Advanced Filter dialog box	(Click Advanced in the Sort & Filter group.) The list and criteria ranges that were previously entered in the dialog box are still there.
3 Select **Copy to another location**	The Copy to box is enabled.
Beside the Copy to box, click	To open the Advanced Filter – Copy to: dialog box.
Select H10	This cell will be the starting point for the filtered result list.
4 Click	To expand the dialog box, as shown in Exhibit 5-7.
Click **OK**	The worksheet displays the filtered list in the specified location.
5 Update and close the workbook	

Topic D: Working with tables

This topic covers the following Microsoft Certified Application Specialist exam objectives for Excel 2007.

#	Objective
1.1.1	**Fill a series** • Fill a series without formatting
2.4.1	**Apply Quick Styles to tables** • Add and remove header rows • Band the rows or columns in a table • Emphasize the first column or last column in a table • Change a table with banded rows to have banded columns
2.4.2	**Add total rows to a table** • Add total rows to a table • Change the summary function of total rows in tables
2.4.3	**Insert and delete rows and columns in tables**
3.3.1	**Create and modify list ranges** • Create a formula that finds the average of displayed values in a filtered list • Create a formula that finds the sum of displayed values in a filtered list • Create a formula that finds the mean or count of displayed values in a filtered list

Tables in Excel

Explanation

When you define a range as a table, Excel formats it and automatically enables filtering. However, Excel also changes the way you add data to the table and the way formulas reference the cells in it.

Creating tables

You can convert a range of data to a table in three ways. Select a cell in the range, and then do any of the following:

- In the Styles group on the Home tab, select a table style from the Format as Table gallery.
- In the Tables group on the Insert tab, click Table.
- Press Ctrl+T.

Do it!

D-1: Creating a table

Here's how	Here's why
1 Open Product information	(In the current unit folder.) This workbook contains sheets with inventory and sales information.
Save the workbook as **My product information**	
2 Select any cell in the range A6:C19	You don't need to select the entire table's range; Excel will attempt to determine it automatically.
3 Activate the Insert tab	
In the Tables group, click **Table**	To open the Create Table dialog box. The selected range is correct.
Click **OK**	To close the dialog box and create the table. By default, Excel applies a built-in style to the table.
4 Update the workbook	

Formatting tables

After creating the table, you can control its formatting by choosing options on the Design tab. This is a Table Tools contextual tab, which is displayed only when you're working with tables.

Options in the Table Style Options group affect how Excel formats the rows and columns:

- The Header Row and Totals Row options determine whether Excel formats the top and bottom rows, and affect how Excel references columns in formulas (as named ranges or as individual cells).
- The First Column and Last Column options determine whether Excel formats the leftmost and rightmost columns differently than the interior columns. Not all table styles apply first- and last-column formatting, so it might not matter whether this option is checked or not.
- The Banded Rows or Banded Columns options apply fill colors to alternating rows or columns, which can make them easier to differentiate.

Choosing a table style from the Table Styles group changes the color scheme and borders. If you formatted the header and/or left column before creating the table, your original formatting will remain applied to those ranges, so only the body of the table will receive new formatting. If you want to override all Table Style Options and return to the formatting you applied before creating the table, select the first table style, None. This table style doesn't initially appear in the Format as Table gallery; you can apply it only after the table has been created.

Do it!

D-2: Formatting a table

Here's how	Here's why
1 Select a single cell in the table	To deselect the table so you can view its formatting without highlighted cells.
2 Verify that the Design tab is active	When you select a cell in a newly created table, Excel automatically activates the Table Tools | Design tab.
In the Table Style Options group, check **First Column**	To emphasize the first column according to the table style. The color changes, and the text becomes bold.
3 In the Table Style Options group, uncheck **Header Row**	To hide the header row.
Uncheck **Banded Rows**	To turn off the alternating row fill colors.
4 Turn on the header row	Check Header Row in the Table Style Options group.
Turn on banded columns	Check Banded Columns in the Table Style Options group.
5 Update the workbook	

Adding to a table

Explanation

When you enter data in a cell adjacent to a table, Excel automatically adds it to the table and formats the top row or left column cell to match. This is an AutoCorrect option, which you can change by clicking the AutoCorrect Options button that appears.

To delete a row or column, you can right-click it and choose Delete, Table Columns or Table Rows. If you want to add or delete several rows and columns at once, you can click Resize Table in the Properties group on the Design tab, and then specify a new range for the table.

Do it!

D-3: Adding and deleting rows and columns

Here's how	Here's why
1 In D6, enter **Total value**	When you press Enter, Excel automatically formats the heading to match those to its left. An AutoCorrect Options button appears.
Click the AutoCorrect Options button as shown	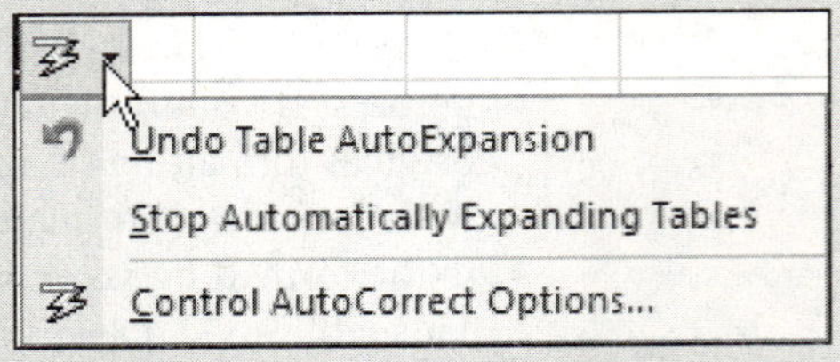 To display options for the automatic action just taken.
Observe the options in the list	You can undo the automatic expansion of the table, stop automatically expanding tables, or control all AutoCorrect options.
Press ESC	To close the list.
2 In A20, type **Cinnamon** and press TAB	To create a new row. Excel automatically expands the table.
In B20, type **10** and press TAB	
In C20, enter **400**	Next, you'll delete the row you just created.
3 Right-click the row	To display a shortcut menu.
Choose **Delete**, **Table Rows**	To delete the new row.
4 Update the workbook	

Structured referencing

Explanation

You can use *structured referencing* in formulas when you create a table. Structured referencing names table columns based on their headings (the values in the top row) and then uses those names in formulas, as shown in Exhibit 5-8.

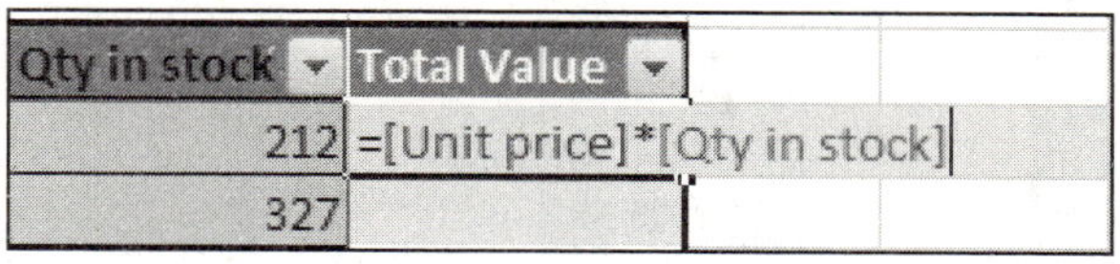

Exhibit 5-8: Structured referencing

To use structured referencing when entering formulas, type "[" to begin a column reference. An AutoComplete list appears, showing names of the table columns to choose from. You can also type a formula with an A1-style cell reference, and Excel won't replace it with a column name, so you can still create traditional formulas if desired.

Additionally, when you press Enter, Excel's default AutoCorrect behavior fills the formula to all other cells in the column. If the formula references a column name, it will appear the same in each cell. So, not only are formulas with structured referencing easier to read, but they are also less prone to errors. Because each cell can contain the exact same formula, it would be more difficult to accidentally change one.

The Totals row

A table can include one special row at the bottom that is designated as the Totals row. Each of its cells can hold a function to summarize the data in the column above. However, instead of using SUM, AVERAGE, or a similar function, formulas in the Totals row are created by default with the SUBTOTAL function. This function, depending on the arguments, can act like SUM, AVERAGE, or other functions.

The reason for this is that the SUBTOTAL function will display the correct value if you apply a filter to one or more columns. For example, if you apply a filter that hides all but two rows, as shown in Exhibit 5-9, the SUBTOTAL function in the Totals row will sum just those values, not all values (including the hidden ones).

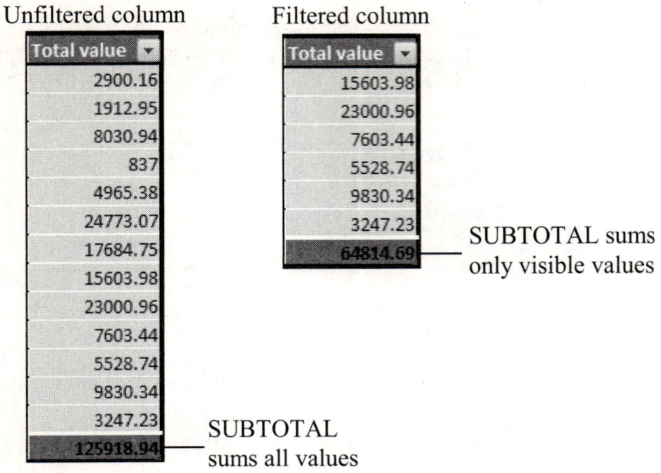

Exhibit 5-9: The SUBTOTAL function in the Totals row operates only on visible cells

Excel creates a Totals row automatically if you select a cell directly below the table and use the AutoSum button to create a formula, or if you check Total Row in the Table Style Options group on the Design tab.

Do it!

D-4: Applying structured referencing

Here's how	Here's why
1 In D7, type **=[**	To begin creating a formula. An AutoComplete list appears, showing the table's column names.
In the list, double-click **Unit Price**	To add a reference to the formula.
Type **]**	To complete the reference
2 Type *****	To enter the multiplication operator.
Complete the formula as shown	fx =[Unit price]*[Qty in stock]
	To calculate the Unit Price multiplied by Qty in stock.
3 Press ENTER	To complete the formula. AutoCorrect adds a formula for each cell in the column.
Observe the formula in D8	The formula in this cell, and in each cell in the column, is the same as the one you entered. All of these formulas refer to the column name, not to individual cells.
Activate the Design tab	(Under Table Tools on the Ribbon.) If necessary.
4 In the Table Style Options group, check **Total Row**	To add a Totals row at the bottom of the table.
Select D20 and observe the formula in it	The formula =SUBTOTAL(109,[Total value]) calculates the sum of the visible cells in the column.
	You'll experiment with other SUBTOTAL types.
5 From the menu to the right of D20, choose **Average**, and then observe the formula	The cell displays the average value. The first argument of the function changes from 109 (which represented Sum) to 101 (which represents Average).
From the menu to the right of D20, choose **Sum**	To reset the formula to calculate the sum.

6	Select C20	
	Activate the Formulas tab	
	Click **AutoSum**	(Click the button, not the menu.) Excel creates a SUBTOTAL function to sum the column. You'll now filter the table to test how the SUBTOTAL functions in the Totals row work.
7	Click the AutoFilter arrow next to Product	To display the sorting and filtering criteria. You'll display only spices with names beginning with the letter B.
8	Choose **Text Filters, Begins With...**	To open the Custom AutoFilter dialog box. In the upper-left list, the first comparison operator, begins with, is selected.
	In the upper-right box, enter **C**	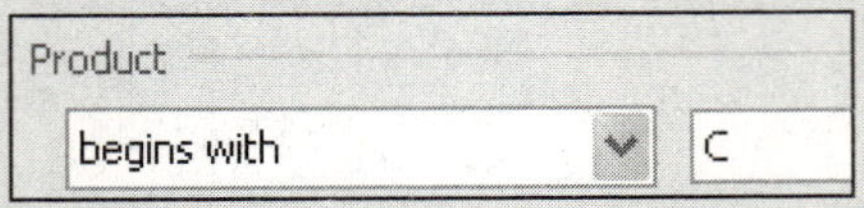
	Click **OK**	To close the dialog box and filter the table so that only spice names beginning with C appear. The formulas in C20 and D20 sum only the visible values.
9	Select D20	
	Calculate the average of the displayed values	Click the arrow next to the cell and choose Average.
10	Calculate the count of Product items in the displayed list	(Select A20, click the arrow next to the cell, and choose Count.) There are six items in the filtered list.
	From the Product column's AutoFilter menu, choose **Clear Filter from "Product"**	To display all values.
11	Update the workbook	

Table names

Explanation

When you create a table, Excel automatically assigns it a name (Table1 for the first table in the workbook, Table2 for the second, etc.). If you create a formula in a cell outside the table, and the formula refers to columns inside the table, Excel will use structured referencing to insert the table name and column name in the formula, as shown in Exhibit 5-10. Formulas in the table don't use the name by default, just as most formulas don't include the worksheet name unless it's necessary.

`fx =AVERAGE(Table1[Unit price])`

Exhibit 5-10: A formula that refers to the Unit price column in the Table1 table.

You can edit the table's name in the Properties group on the Table Tools | Design. Formulas that refer to the table are updated automatically when you change the table name.

Do it!

D-5: Naming tables

Here's how	Here's why
1 In B4, type **=AVERAGE(**	Don't press Enter.
2 Select B7:B19	To select the Unit price column. The formula appears as shown in Exhibit 5-10.
Press ENTER	To enter the formula. If you AutoFill the cell to the right, the next cell's formula will contain the adjacent table column's name.
3 AutoFill B4 one cell to the right	To copy the formula to C4.
From the AutoFill Options menu, choose **Fill Without Formatting**	To remove the currency formatting from C4.
Select C4 and observe the formula	The formula references Table1[Qty in stock].
	You'll now change the table name to see the effect it has on the formulas.
4 Select any cell in the table	
Activate the Design tab	
5 In the Properties group, edit the Table Name box to read **InventoryTable**	Do not enter a space between words.
Select B4	The formula now references InventoryTable instead of Table1.
6 Update the workbook	

Functions tabulating row values

Explanation

Some Excel functions "expect" the arguments to be a range of cells. For example, the SUM function acts upon a range of values, not just one. Therefore, an argument such as a table column name is valid for the SUM function; `=SUM([January])` can be the equivalent of `=SUM(C5:C14)`.

At times, however, you might want to use a table column name in a function, but reference only a single row. For example, if you want to sum the values across a table row, you don't want to sum all the values for all of the rows. To address this issue, you can insert a special `[#This Row]` argument in formulas.

Exhibit 5-11 shows this argument in a cell that sums the values in one row of the January-through-April columns of a table.

```
=SUM(Table2[[#This Row],[January]:[April]])
```

Exhibit 5-11: A function to sum a single row across table cells should include the [#This Row] argument

Although you can type this argument, the easiest way to insert it is to use the AutoSum button to create the formula. Excel will then insert the argument automatically.

Do it!

D-6: Creating functions with [#This Row]

Here's how	Here's why
1 Activate the Sales sheet	You'll convert this sheet's data to a table and then add a formula in a new column.
Select a cell in A4:F14 and define the range as a table	Activate the Insert tab and click Table in the Tables group. Click OK to accept the defaults.
2 In G4, enter **Total**	Excel adds this column to the table automatically.
3 Activate the Home tab	If necessary.
With G5 selected, click **AutoSum** in the Editing group	To add a formula that sums the values from the January-through-April columns.
Press ENTER	To create the formula and automatically fill it to the remaining rows in the column.
	Next, you'll see the effect of removing the special [#This row] argument.
4 Edit the formula to read **=SUM(Table2[[January]:[April]])**	Delete the text "[#This Row]" from the formula.
Press ENTER	When you press Enter, all cells in the column display the result $563,768, because all formulas are summing all of the values in the columns, not just the values to the cell's left.
On the Quick Access toolbar, click 	To return to the original formula in the filled cells.
Click 	To delete the remaining formula.
5 Update and close the workbook	

Unit summary: Lists and tables

Topic A

In this topic, you learned about the structure of a **list**. You learned that a list displays related data in a concise and logical manner. You learned that the rows in a list are called **records** and the columns are called **fields**. You also learned that **field names** are the column headings that appear in the first row of a list.

Topic B

In this topic, you learned how to **sort** a list in ascending or descending order based on the values in a column. You also learned how to use the **AutoFilter** feature to filter a list to show only those rows that meet certain criteria. Finally, you learned how to sort and filter a list by using fill color and other cell attributes as the criteria.

Topic C

In this topic, you learned how to use the **Custom AutoFilter** dialog box to filter a list based on multiple criteria. You learned how to use a **criteria range** and the **Advanced Filter** command to specify more complex criteria. You also learned how to copy a filtered list to another location in the worksheet.

Topic D

In this topic, you learned how to **create tables** to simplify the tasks of formatting data, adding data, and creating formulas. You applied **structured referencing** in formulas to include references to column names instead of A1-style ranges. You then **renamed a table**, and you used the **[#This Row] argument** in a SUM function with column-name references to total only the cells in the same row.

Independent practice activity

In this activity, you'll sort and AutoFilter the values in a list. You'll also use a criteria range to filter the list, and copy the results to another place in the worksheet. Last, you'll define a range as a table, and apply structured referencing to create formulas that refer to column names.

1 Open Practice list and save it as **My practice list**.

2 Sort the list by Product code in ascending order. (*Hint*: Activate the Data tab, select the first record in the Product Code field, and click Sort Smallest to Largest.)

3 Sort the list first by Re-order level (Kg) in descending order, and then by Product name in ascending order. (*Hint*: Click the Sort button to open the Sort dialog box.)

4 Use AutoFilter to display only those records for the supplier Cedric Stone. Then, display all records again.

5 Display only those records for the suppliers Cedric Stone or Bill Johnson. Then, display all records again. (*Hint*: Click the AutoFilter button next to Suppliers and choose **Text Filters**.)

6 Create a filtered list to display only those records where the re-order level is greater than 2000 and less than 3500. (*Hint:* Click the AutoFilter button next to Re-order level (Kg) and choose **Number Filters**.)

7 Compare your result with Exhibit 5-12.

8 Turn off AutoFilter.

9 Use the criteria labels in F3:G3 to create a criteria range to display only those records where the re-order level for Cedric Stone is greater than 2000, or the re-order level for Bill Johnson is greater than 3000. (*Hint*: In F4, enter **Cedric Stone**; in G4, enter **>2000**, and so on. Select a cell in the original range and click Advanced in the Sort & Filter group. Select F3:G5 as the criteria range.)

10 Copy the filtered result to a range starting with I3 so that you can view the filtered and unfiltered lists simultaneously. (*Hint*: Open the Advanced Filter dialog box and select "Copy to another location.")

11 Adjust column widths and row heights as necessary in the resulting range, and compare your results with Exhibit 5-13.

12 Activate the Bonus sales sheet.

13 Define the data range as a table, and turn off the banded rows.

14 Add a Totals column starting in F4.

15 In the Totals column, create formulas to sum the four quarter values in each row. (*Hint:* Use the AutoSum button to insert the necessary arguments into the formula automatically.)

16 Create a Totals row, and choose the SUM function from the list in cells B15:E15. (*Hint:* Activate the Design tab, and in the Table Style Options group, check Totals Row.) Compare your table to Exhibit 5-14.

17 Name the table **BonusSales**.

18 Update and close the workbook.

3	Product name	Product code	Suppliers	Re-order level(K
14	Basil leaf (ground)	20	Richie Hamond	3200
15	Caraway seed (ground)	14	Bill Johnson	3200
16	Cardamom seed (whole)	8	Anthony Felix	3000
17	Chives	31	Paul Michelin	3000
18	Cinnamon (ground) extra high oil (2x)	12	Anthony Felix	3000
19	Catnip leaf	26	Charles Nought	2900
20	Anise seeds	18	Bill Johnson	2800
21	Coarse kosher salt flakes	36	Henry Sanders	2800
22	Cassia	2	Garry Harper	2600
23	Anise	32	Cedric Stone	2500
24	Chinese star anise (whole)	27	Dennis Linekar	2500
25	Celery seed (ground)	12	Andy Howard	2300
26	Caraway seed (whole)	16	Michael Smith	2100
27	Cloves (whole)	35	Charly Bobbit	2100

Exhibit 5-12: The My practice list worksheet after Step 6 of the independent practice activity

Product name	Product code	Suppliers	Re-order level(Kg)
Anise	32	Cedric Stone	2500
Caraway seed (ground)	14	Bill Johnson	3200
Cardamom seed (ground)	5	Cedric Stone	4000

Exhibit 5-13: The My practice list worksheet after Step 11

Product	Q	Q	Q	Q	Tot
Anise Seeds	$534	$423	$521	$625	$2,103
Asafoetida Powder	$654	$634	$326	$754	$2,368
Basil Leaf (Whole)	$6,778	$6,760	$4,568	$7,834	$25,940
Bay Leaf (Whole)	$233	$532	$525	$652	$1,942
Caraway Seed (Whole)	$354	$633	$422	$255	$1,664
Cardamom Seed (Whole)	$255	$525	$252	$624	$1,656
Cardamom Seed (Ground)	$422	$642	$642	$624	$2,330
Catnip Leaf	$854	$364	$474	$743	$2,435
Celery Seed (Whole)	$3,634	$6,344	$6,423	$2,546	$18,947
Chamomile Flowers	$356	$634	$632	$743	$2,365
Total	$14,074	$17,491	$14,785	$15,400	$61,750

Exhibit 5-14: The Bonus Sales worksheet after Step 16

Review questions

1 What is a list?

2 List the steps you would use to sort a list.

3 What menu choice will display the AutoFilter arrows next to each column heading?

4 What is a criteria range?

5 List the steps you would use to keep an original list intact and place a copy of the filtered list somewhere else in the same worksheet.

6 How can formulas in a range defined as a table differ from those in a typical range?

7 Name two advantages of structured referencing.

Unit 6

Web and Internet features

Unit time: 30 minutes

Complete this unit, and you'll know how to:

A Save a workbook as a Web page, and use the AutoRepublish feature to keep the Web version of a workbook updated.

B Add and remove hyperlinks in a worksheet.

C Save a workbook as a PDF file, and send a workbook via e-mail.

Topic A: Saving workbooks as Web pages

This topic covers the following Microsoft Certified Application Specialist exam objective for Excel 2007.

#	Objective
5.4.2	**Using the correct format, save a workbook as a template, a Web page, a macro-enabled document, or another appropriate document.** • Save as a Web page

Excel and the Web

Explanation

By saving your workbooks, worksheets, and charts as Web pages, you can make them available to anyone who has a browser and access to the Internet or your corporate intranet. You can even provide some of Excel's functionality to people who don't have access to Excel, permitting these and other users to update and manipulate data through their browsers.

Making Web commands available

Web options are not displayed in the default Excel configuration. You can use the Excel Options dialog box to add Web options to the Quick Access toolbar.

Do it!

A-1: Making Web commands available

Here's how	Here's why
1 On the right side of the Quick Access toolbar, click the arrow and choose **More Commands...**	To open the Excel Options dialog box with the Customization settings displayed. You'll make a Web command available by adding it to the Quick Access toolbar.
2 Under Customize Quick Access Toolbar, verify that "For all documents (default)" is selected	You'll make these changes effective for all workbooks.
3 Under Choose commands from, click the arrow and select **All Commands**	(Scroll to the bottom of the list.) To display all available commands.
Select **Web Page Preview**	Near the bottom of the alphabetized list.
Click **Add**	To add a button for the Web Page Preview command to the Quick Access toolbar.
4 Click **OK**	To save the changes and close the Excel Options dialog box.
5 Observe the Quick Access toolbar	 The command button you added appears on the right side of the toolbar.

Saving workbooks

Explanation

You can save a selection, worksheet, or workbook as a Web page by using the Save As dialog box, shown in Exhibit 6-1. From the Save as type list, select Web Page, and then click OK. This saves the page with the file-name extension .htm. All of the graphics and images in the document are saved in an associated folder. You can also select Single File Web Page to save the page with the file-name extension .mht. This file type embeds the document's graphics and images directly in the Web page.

Previewing Web pages in a browser

You can preview Web pages in a Web browser before publishing them. When you open a Web page in a browser, that page is temporarily saved in the Windows directory. After you close the browser, the temporary files are deleted automatically. To preview a Web page in a Web browser, click the Web Page Preview button that you added to the Quick Access toolbar. Your default Web browser will be launched automatically with your Web page.

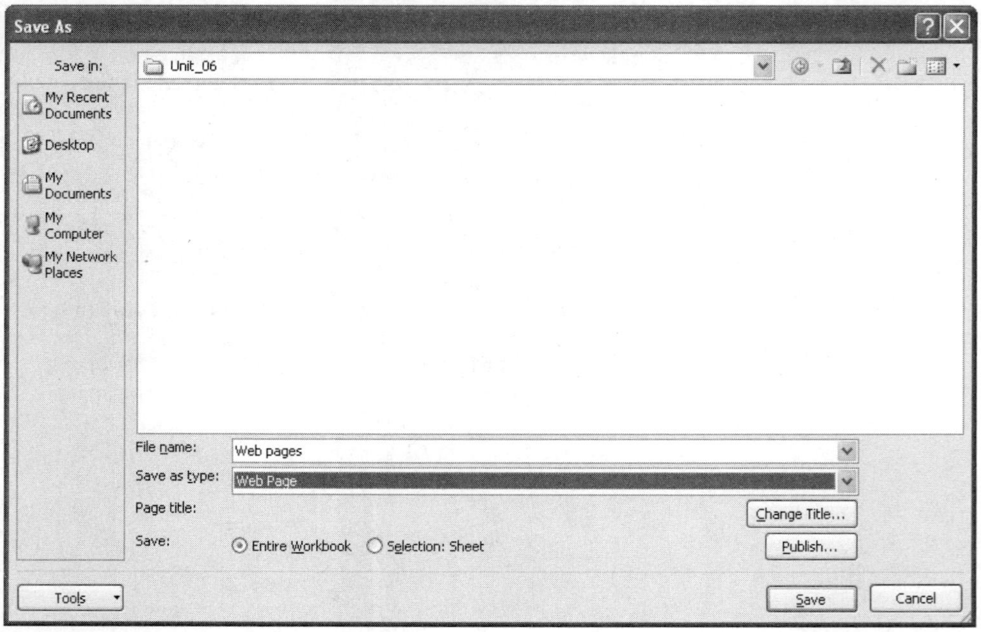

Exhibit 6-1: Using the Save As dialog box to save a workbook as a Web page

Do it!

A-2: Saving a workbook as a Web page

Here's how	Here's why
1 Open Web pages	(From the current unit folder.) This workbook contains a sheet with five years of revenue figures for Outlander Spices. The sheet also contains an embedded chart.
2 Click 	(You added the Web Page Preview button to the Quick Access toolbar in the previous activity.) Internet Explorer opens, showing a preview of how the worksheet will look as a Web document. Though not all features of a published worksheet are available in the preview, it will give you an idea of how the worksheet will look when viewed in a browser.
Click 	To close Internet Explorer.
3 Open the Save As dialog box	
From the Save as type list, select **Web Page**	To save the file as a Web page. When you save a worksheet as a Web page, the Save As dialog box contains several unique options, as shown in Exhibit 6-1. You can choose to save the entire workbook or save only a selection, such as the current sheet or a selected range. You can also add a Web page title.
Save the file as **My web pages**	To save the workbook as a Web page. A message box appears to tell you that the Web page version of this file might contain features that are not compatible with the original.
Click **Yes**	To close the message box, if necessary.
4 Start Windows Explorer	Choose Start, All Programs, Accessories, Windows Explorer.
Double-click My web pages	(In the current unit folder.) To open it in Internet Explorer.
5 Click the yellow Information bar in the browser and choose **Allow Blocked Content...**	To remove security restrictions on this page. A Security Warning box prompts you to confirm that you'll let the page run active content.
Click **Yes**	To close the Security Warning box.
6 Close Internet Explorer	

Publishing a Web page

Explanation

To control more aspects of how your worksheets or elements of them will behave on the Web, you can publish them. To publish a workbook or a part of it:

1. Open the Save As dialog box and choose Web Page as the file type.
2. Click the Publish button to open the Publish as Web Page dialog box.
3. From the Choose list, select the part you want to publish.
4. Click Publish to publish the worksheet and open the page in Internet Explorer, as shown in Exhibit 6-2.

The AutoRepublish feature

The AutoRepublish feature ensures that each time you save the data in a workbook that's published on the Web, the Web pages are also updated automatically. To use this feature, check the "AutoRepublish every time this workbook is saved" option in the Publish as Web Page dialog box. You can also disable AutoRepublish temporarily or permanently.

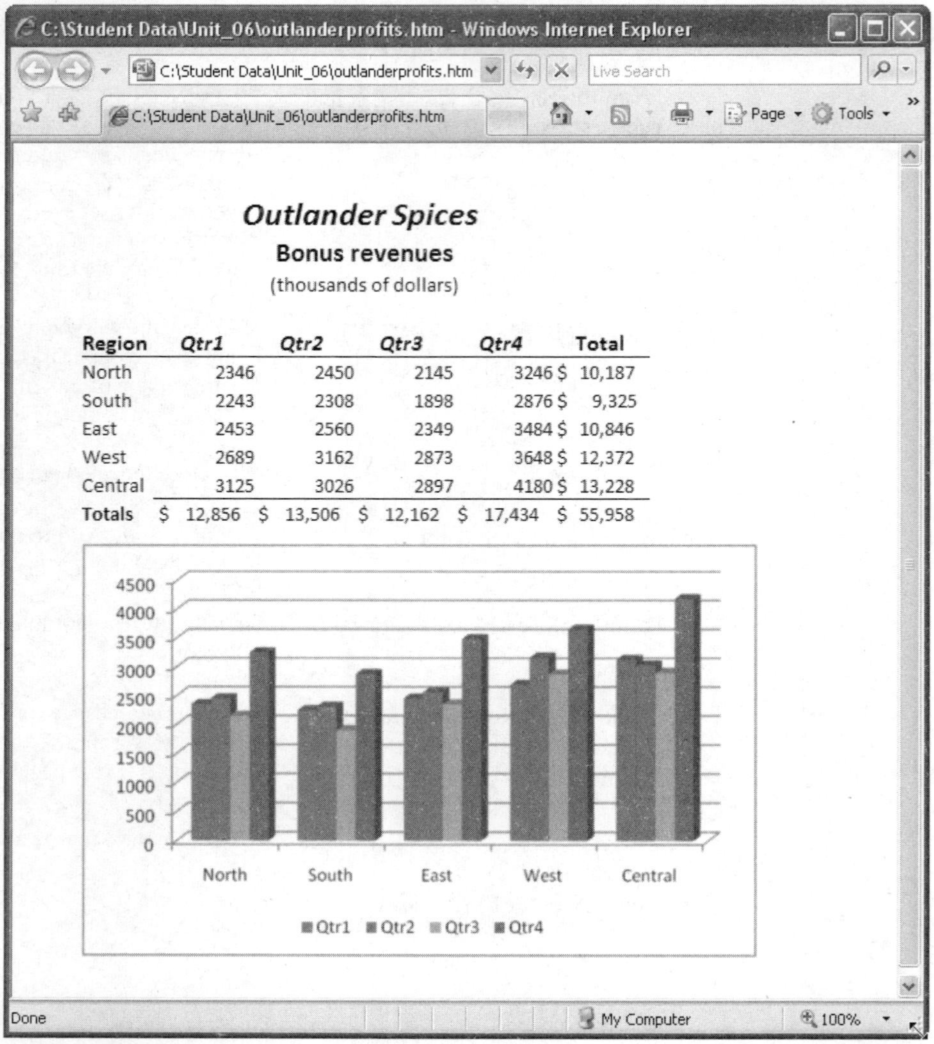

Exhibit 6-2: A published worksheet in Internet Explorer

Do it!

A-3: Using the Publish as Web Page dialog box

Here's how	Here's why
1 Open the Save As dialog box	
From the Save as type list, select **Web Page**	(If necessary.) To display the Web page options.
Click **Publish**	To open the Publish as Web Page dialog box.
2 Edit the File name box to read **outlanderprofits.htm**, as shown	 You'll publish the Web page, on your own hard drive, with the file name outlanderprofits. To make the file available to other users, you would need to publish it to a Web server or some other computer to which other users have access.
Check **AutoRepublish every time this workbook is saved**	To update the Web page with changes you make in your Excel file.
Check **Open published web page in browser**	(If necessary.) To get an immediate confirmation that the update works when you publish it.
3 Click **Publish**	To publish the worksheet on your own hard drive and open the page in Internet Explorer. Your screen should look similar to Exhibit 6-2.
4 Close Internet Explorer	
5 Move the legend to the top of the chart	Click the chart to display the Chart Tools, and then activate the Layout tab. Click Legend and choose Show Legend at Top.
6 Update the workbook	A message box appears.
Click **Yes**	To keep the workbook in this format. Another dialog box opens.
Select **Enable the AutoRepublish feature**	To make your worksheet changes appear on the Web page.
Click **OK**	To close the Microsoft Excel dialog box.
7 Open outlanderprofits.htm in Internet Explorer	Notice that the change you made in Excel appears here as well.
Close Internet Explorer	
Close the workbook	

Topic B: Using hyperlinks

This topic covers the following Microsoft Certified Application Specialist exam objective for Excel 2007.

#	Objective
2.3.8	Insert, modify, and remove hyperlinks

Hyperlinks and URLs

Explanation

A *hyperlink* is any text or graphic that has been formatted to include a Uniform Resource Locator (URL). *URLs* are addresses of files on the Internet. When you click a hyperlink, your browser will load the file to which the URL points.

Inserting a hyperlink in a worksheet

To insert a hyperlink in a worksheet:

1. Select the cell where you want the hyperlink to appear.
2. Activate the Insert tab.
3. In the Links group, click Hyperlink to open the Insert Hyperlink dialog box.
4. Specify the text you want the link to display. This can be any text (but preferably something descriptive). It does not have to be the name of the file or its URL.
5. Specify the file or Web page to which you want the hyperlink to point. You can browse for a file or a Web page, or choose from recently used files, recently visited Web pages, or previously inserted links.
6. Click OK.

You can then click the hyperlink to load the specified file in your browser. If you save a worksheet as a Web page and that sheet contains a hyperlink, that link will work within the Web page as well.

Do it!

B-1: Inserting and editing hyperlinks

Here's how	Here's why
1 Create a new blank workbook	You'll insert a hyperlink that points to the Web page you just created.
2 Select A1	If necessary.
3 Activate the Insert tab	
4 In the Links group, click **Hyperlink**	 To open the Insert Hyperlink dialog box.
5 In the Text to display box, enter **Outlander Spices profits**	The hyperlink will display this text.
Click **Recent Files**, as shown	 To display a list of recently opened files.
6 Select **outlanderprofits.htm**	It should be one of the first files listed.
Click **OK**	To insert the hyperlink in A1.
7 Widen column A to fit the hyperlink, as shown	 (Double-click the column border in the heading row to autofit the cell to the contents.) This is done so that the entire text string will be available for users to click.
8 Point to the hyperlink	The shape of the pointer changes to a hand.
Click the mouse button	A Security Notice appears, reminding you that hyperlinks can be harmful to your computer and asking whether you want to continue.
Click **Yes**	To close the message box and open the Outlanderprofits Web page in Internet Explorer.
Close Internet Explorer	

9	Open the Save As dialog box	
	From the Save as type list, select **Web Page**	
	Edit the File name box to read **mylink**	
10	Click **Save**	To save the file as a Web page. A message box may appear, stating that the file may contain features that are not compatible with Web pages.
	Click **Yes**	To save in this format while deleting any incompatible features, if necessary.
11	Open mylink in Internet Explorer	
	Click the hyperlink, as shown	 To navigate to the outlanderprofits Web page.
	Close Internet Explorer	
12	Edit the formula bar to read **Outlander Spices profits by region**	To edit the hyperlink.
	Press ENTER	
13	Update the Web page	Click the Save button.
14	Open mylink in Internet Explorer	The hyperlink displays the edited text.
	Click the hyperlink	To open the outlanderprofits Web page.
	Close Internet Explorer	
15	Delete the hyperlink	(A1 should be active.) Press Delete.
	Update the workbook and save the formatting	
	Open mylink in Internet Explorer	The hyperlink is deleted.
16	Close Internet Explorer	
	Close the workbooks	You do not need to save changes.

Topic C: Distributing workbooks

This topic covers the following Microsoft Certified Application Specialist exam objective for Excel 2007.

#	Objective
5.4.2	**Using the correct format, save a workbook as a template, a Web page, a macro-enabled document, or another appropriate document.** • Save as a PDF

Sharing workbooks

Explanation

There are other ways to share workbooks apart from publishing them to the Web. You can save a workbook in PDF format and/or send it to someone by e-mail.

PDF stands for *Portable Document Format*, a file format developed by Adobe Systems. It is a commonly used format for files placed on the Web and for file-sharing between users. The PDF format preserves document formatting across disparate computer systems, and ensures that what is viewed online or printed appears as originally intended.

You can save a workbook as a PDF file by downloading and installing the Microsoft Save as PDF or XPS add-in. Then, click the Office Button and point to Save As to view choices in the Save As menu. Click PDF or XPS to open the Publish as PDF or XPS dialog box. Here, you can choose among several options, as shown in Exhibit 6-3.

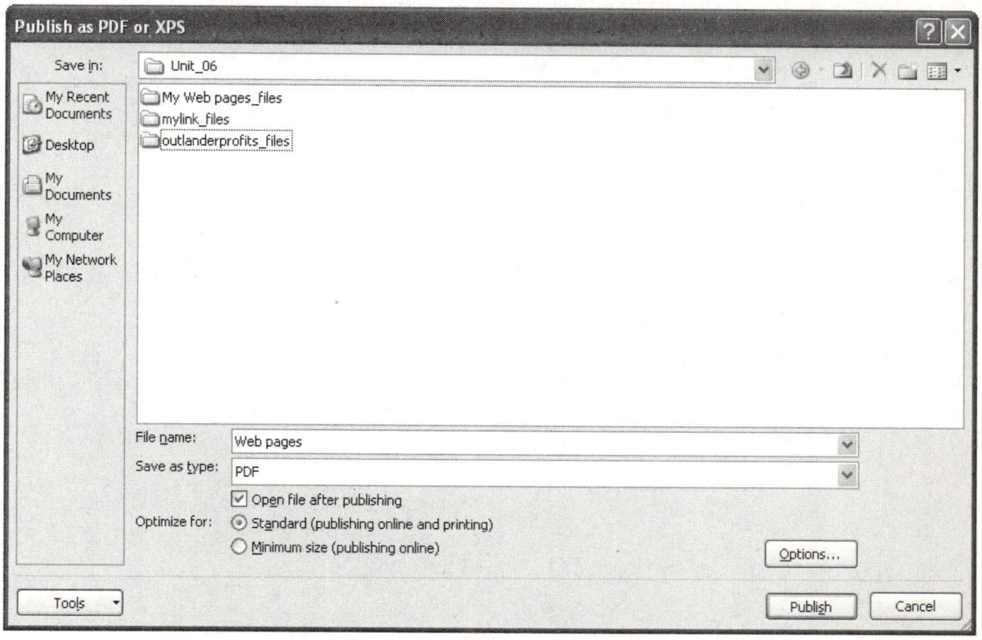

Exhibit 6-3: The Publish as PDF or XPS dialog box

Do it!

C-1: Saving a workbook as a PDF file

Here's how	Here's why
1 Open Web pages	
2 Click 	To display the Office menu.
3 Choose **Save As**, **PDF or XPS**	To open the Publish as PDF or XPS dialog box, as shown in Exhibit 6-3.
4 Edit the file name to read **My PDF file**	
5 Click **Options**	To display the options available for publishing as a PDF file. You can publish the entire workbook, the current worksheet, or a selection. You can include or exclude certain document information.
Click **OK**	To accept the default options for the file.
6 Verify that "Open file after publishing" is checked	
Click **Publish**	To publish the workbook as a PDF file. The file opens in Adobe Reader. Notice that the worksheet's formatting has been retained.
7 Close Adobe Reader	
Close Web pages	Do not save changes.

Sending workbooks via e-mail

Explanation

To send a workbook by e-mail, both you (the sender) and the recipient must have compatible e-mail programs and must have this version of Excel installed. The exact steps for sending the e-mail message will vary depending on your e-mail program, but this option works with most standard e-mail programs.

Options for sharing workbooks through e-mail

You can share a workbook through e-mail either as an attachment or in HTML format in the body of the message. (To do the latter, you need Outlook 2000 or higher.) Here's how to send a workbook via e-mail:

1. Click the Office Button and choose Send, Email. An e-mail message opens, with the current workbook inserted in the message as an attachment.
2. Specify the address(es), and send the message.

Do it!

C-2: Using e-mail to share a workbook

Questions and answers
1 What options do you have for sending a workbook via e-mail?
2 What do you need to send a worksheet in the body of an e-mail message?

Unit summary: Web and Internet features

Topic A In this topic, you learned how to add the **Web Page Preview command** to the Quick Access toolbar and how to use this command to see the worksheet in a browser. You also learned how save a worksheet as a **Web page** by choosing Web Page as the file type in the Save As dialog box. You then used the **Publish as Web Page** dialog box to save a worksheet with an embedded chart as a Web page. You also learned how to use the **AutoRepublish** feature.

Topic B In this topic, you learned how to insert and edit **hyperlinks** in a workbook. You learned that clicking a hyperlink opens a Web page in a browser.

Topic C In this topic, you learned how to save a workbook as a **PDF** file, and how to send a workbook through **e-mail**.

Independent practice activity

In this activity, you'll publish workbooks as Web pages. You'll use the AutoRepublish feature to update a published Web page when you change the source workbook. You'll create a hyperlink in a workbook, publish as a Web page, and observe the action of the hyperlink.

1 Open Practice web 1 and save it as **My practice web 1**. This file contains bonus sales data for Outlander Spices' southern region.

2 Publish the workbook as a Web page. Name it **mysouthernregion.htm**, activate the AutoRepublish feature, and save the file in the current unit folder.

3 Open the Web page in your browser (if necessary); then close it.

4 Change the value in C6 to **7000** and update the workbook. To verify that the Web page was republished, view it in the browser. Then close the browser.

5 In Excel, open Practice web 2 and save it as **My practice web 2**. This file contains the northern region's sales data.

6 In A13, insert a hyperlink to the mysouthernregion.htm Web page. Make **Southern region** the text displayed for the hyperlink.

7 Publish My practice web 2 as a Web page. Name it **mynorthernregion.htm**, activate the AutoRepublish feature, and save the file in the current unit folder.

8 Open mynorthernregion.htm in your browser (if necessary).

9 Use the hyperlink to open mysouthernregion.htm, and then close the browser.

10 Update My practice web 2, enabling the AutoRepublish feature. Close the workbook.

11 In A13 of the My practice web 1 workbook, insert a hyperlink to the mynorthernregion.htm Web page. Make **Northern region** the text displayed for the hyperlink.

12 Update the workbook.

13 Open mysouthernregion.htm in your browser, and compare it to Exhibit 6-4.

14 Use the hyperlink to load the mynorthernregion.htm Web page, and use the link in that page to reload mysouthernregion.htm.

15 Close the browser.

16 Open Practice web 1 and publish it as a PDF file.

17 View the file in Adobe Reader, and then close the reader.

18 Update and close the workbooks.

Outlander Spices

Bonus sales report for the southern region

Name	Emp #	Qtr1	Qtr2	Qtr3	Qtr4	Total	Comm
Michael Bobrow	16	7000	8732	7722	3990	$ 27,460	$ 1,098
Karen Anderson	22	8765	3224	8865	4936	$ 25,812	$ 1,032
James Hanover	27	3440	3958	5784	4601	$ 17,810	$ 712
Kelly Palmatier	29	3716	8917	5662	3324	$ 21,648	$ 866
Totals		$ 22,921	$ 24,831	$ 28,033	$ 16,851	$ 92,730	$ 3,709

Northern region

Exhibit 6-4: The contents of the southernregion.htm Web page after Step 13 of the independent practice activity

Review questions

1 When you save a worksheet as a Web page, you can save the file as a Single File Web Page with the extension .mht. When you use this option, how are the graphics and images stored?

2 When you save a worksheet as a Web Page and save the file in an HTML format, how are the graphics and images stored?

3 How can you preview a Web page in a Web browser?

4 List the steps you would use to publish a workbook.

5 What is a hyperlink?

6 What does PDF stand for?

7 What is a primary advantage of the PDF format?

Unit 7

Advanced charting

Unit time: 30 minutes

Complete this unit, and you'll know how to:

A Adjust the scale of a chart, and format data points.

B Create combination charts and trendlines to highlight different kinds of data.

C Add and format graphic elements to highlight a specific portion of a chart, and add a picture to a worksheet.

Topic A: Chart formatting options

This topic covers the following Microsoft Certified Application Specialist exam objective for Excel 2007.

#	Objective
4.2.1	**Add and remove chart elements** • Percentages

Working with formatting options

Explanation

Excel provides many formatting options for charts. You can use these options to represent or interpret complex data. For example, you can change the scale of a chart or format specific data points.

When you create or work with a chart, the Chart Tools appear. Design, Layout, and Format tabs are added to the Ribbon.

Changing a chart's scale

You can change the scale of a chart to:

- Adjust the range of values on each axis.
- Change the way the values appear on each axis.
- Specify the intervals at which the values appear.
- Set the point at which one axis crosses another.

To change the scale of a chart, select the value axis and activate the Layout tab. In the Labels group, click Axes, and choose Primary Vertical Axis, More Primary Vertical Axis Options to open the Format Axis dialog box. Activate the Axis Options page, shown in Exhibit 5-1. The following table describes some of the options available on the Axis Options page:

Option	Specifies...
Minimum	The lowest value on the value axis.
Maximum	The highest value on the value axis.
Major unit	The intervals for major tick marks and major gridlines on the value axis.
Minor unit	The intervals for minor tick marks and minor gridlines on the value axis.

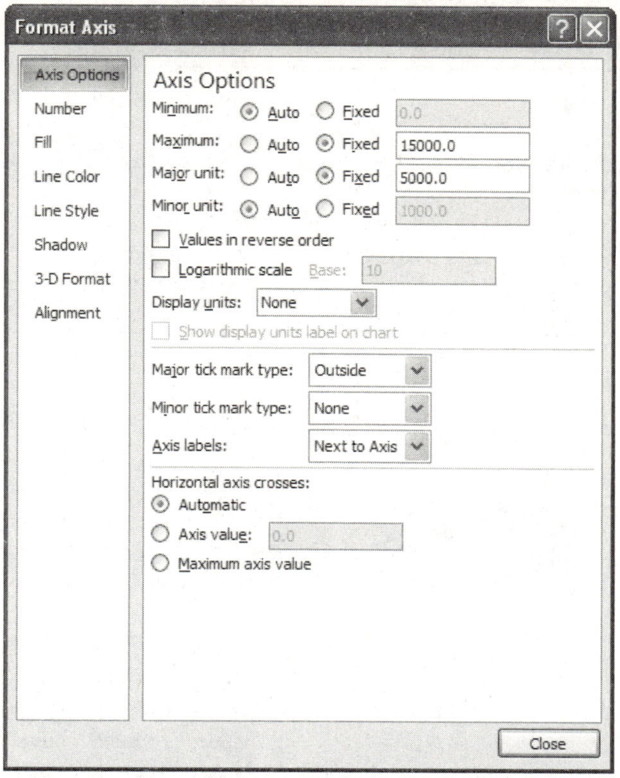

Exhibit 7-1: Options on the Axis Options page in the Format Axis dialog box

Do it!

A-1: Adjusting the scale of a chart

Here's how	Here's why
1 Open Charts	From the current unit folder.
Save the workbook as **My charts**	In the current unit folder.
2 Verify that the Scale worksheet is active	It contains the quarterly bonus sales report for five Outlander Spices salespeople.

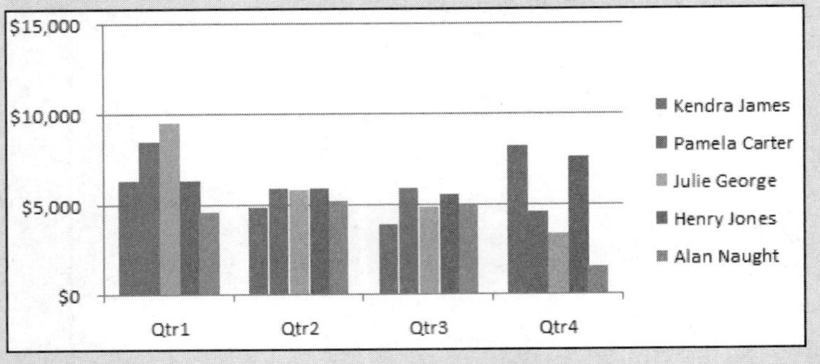

Here's how	Here's why
	On the chart, the value axis displays a maximum value of $15,000. The interval between the values is $5,000. This scale is not suitable because the value axis is too large, making the columns seem small and minimizing the difference between data points.
3 Select the chart	The Chart Tools appear on the Ribbon.
4 Activate the Layout tab	
In the Axes group, click **Axes** and choose **Primary Vertical Axis**, **More Primary Vertical Axis Options…**	To open the Format Axis dialog box.
In the left-hand pane, select **Axis Options**	(If necessary.) You'll change the scale of the value axis.
5 Next to Maximum, select **Fixed**	(If necessary.) You'll override the current maximum value with your own fixed value.
Edit the Maximum box to read **10000**	Excel might reformat the values here with a single decimal place. The value you enter might appear as 10000.0.
Set the Major unit to **2000**	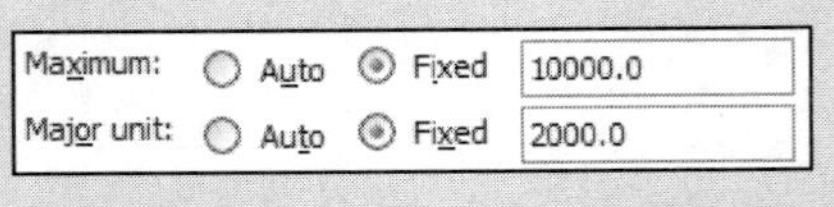 Next to Major Unit, select Fixed, if necessary. Then edit the box to read 2000.

6 Click **Close**

To close the Format Axis dialog box and apply the new scale settings.

Deselect the chart

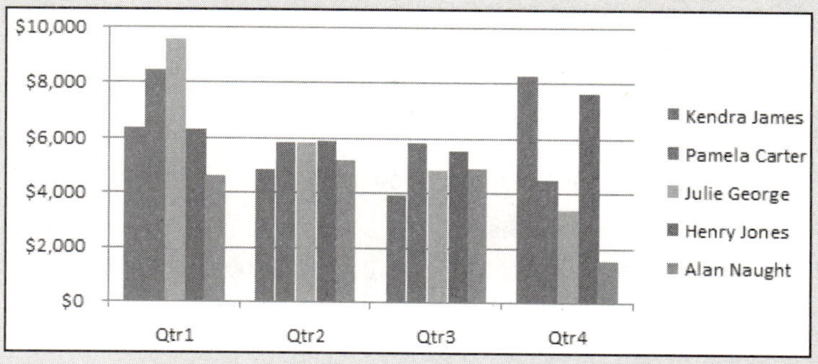

The value axis now displays a maximum value of $10,000. The major tick marks occur at intervals of $2,000. This scale is more appropriate for the data.

7 Update the workbook

Formatting data points

Explanation

You can change the appearance of data points to make them stand out or make them easier to understand. You can add or remove labels, percentages, or leader lines. A *leader line* is a line from the data label to its associated data point. In a pie chart, you can change the orientation of the first slice or pull out a slice to make it stand out.

Labeling data points

To add a label to a data point:

1. Select the data point you want to label.
2. Activate the Layout tab.
3. In the Labels group, click Data Labels and choose More Data Label Options to open the Format Data Label dialog box.
4. Activate the Label Options page, shown in Exhibit 5-3.
5. Select a label option and click OK.

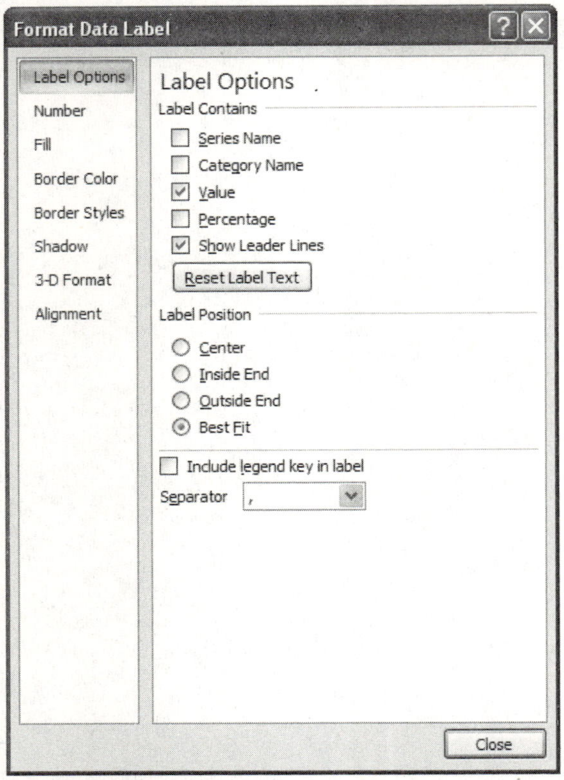

Exhibit 7-2: Label options in the Format Data Label dialog box

Formatting pie charts

You can format a pie chart to draw attention to specific data points. You can rotate the chart, and you can pull out a slice by dragging it away from the pie. The individual slice can be formatted to make it stand out from the rest of the chart.

Do it!

A-2: Formatting a data point

Here's how	Here's why
1 Activate the Datapoint worksheet	This worksheet contains the total yearly bonus sales report for several products. The pie chart represents a breakdown of sales by product.
2 Select the slice representing cinnamon sales	(Click the pie and then click the largest slice.) The Chart Tools tabs appear. You'll add a label to this data point.
3 Activate the Layout tab	
In the Labels group, click **Data Labels** and choose **More Data Label Options…**	 To open the Format Data Label dialog box. By default, Label Options is selected, as shown in Exhibit 5-4.
4 Under Label Contains, clear **Value**	You'll label the slice representing cinnamon sales as a percentage of the total.
Under Label Contains, check **Percentage**	
Under Label Position, select **Outside End**	To place the data label just outside the slice.
5 In the left pane, select **Number**	
From the Category list, select **Percentage**	To format the number as a percentage.
Edit the Decimal places box to read **0**	If necessary.
Click **Close**	To close the dialog box and add the label.
6 Observe the chart	The new data label, representing the total value of cinnamon sales, appears outside the pie slice.
Click anywhere in the chart	To deselect the slice and data label.
Point to the cinnamon slice	A ScreenTip appears, showing the total value of cinnamon sales and the percentage of total product sales it represents.
7 Select the slice representing cinnamon sales	You'll make other changes to the slice.
8 Activate the Format tab	

9	In the Current Selection group, click **Format Selection**	To open the Format Data Point dialog box. Series Options is selected by default.
10	Set the “Angle of first slice” value to **195**	(Drag the slider or type the value in the box.) To rotate the pie chart so that the cinnamon slice occupies a 9 o’clock position.
	Set the Point Explosion value to approximately **20%**	To pull out the slice representing cinnamon sales so that it is separate from the rest of the pie chart. This will make this data point stand out from the others.
11	In the left pane, select **3-D Format**	You’ll give the slice some depth.
	Under Bevel, click as shown	 You’ll create a special effect for the slice.
	Select the indicated bevel option	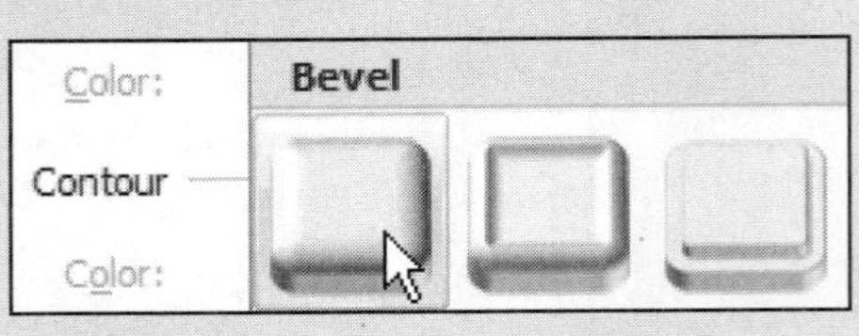 To create the effect of a raised circle.
12	Click **Close**	To close the dialog box.
	Deselect the slice	The slice now has a beveled edge to make it even more distinct from the other slices.
13	Update the workbook	

Topic B: Combination charts

This topic covers the following Microsoft Certified Application Specialist exam objective for Excel 2007.

#	Objective
4.1.2	**Select appropriate chart types to represent data sources**
	• Create a chart that shows a trend over time
	• Create a chart that compares two data sets over time

When to combine chart types

Explanation

You can combine two or more chart types in a single chart, called a *combination chart.* For example, you can combine a column chart with a line chart. Other chart combinations are also possible. You can use combination charts when you want to represent a wider range of information or when you want to highlight a series or the contrast between series. You can also graphically represent variations in data by using trendlines.

Changing chart types and adding axes

At times, you might need to show two kinds of information on the same chart. For example, in Exhibit 5-3, the columns show expense and sales figures, measured in thousands of dollars, while the line shows profit figures, which are percentages. You can create combination charts by applying a secondary axis to one or more data series. You can also change the chart type for that data series to make it stand out from the rest of the chart. This is especially useful if the values for that data series are very different from the values for the other data series.

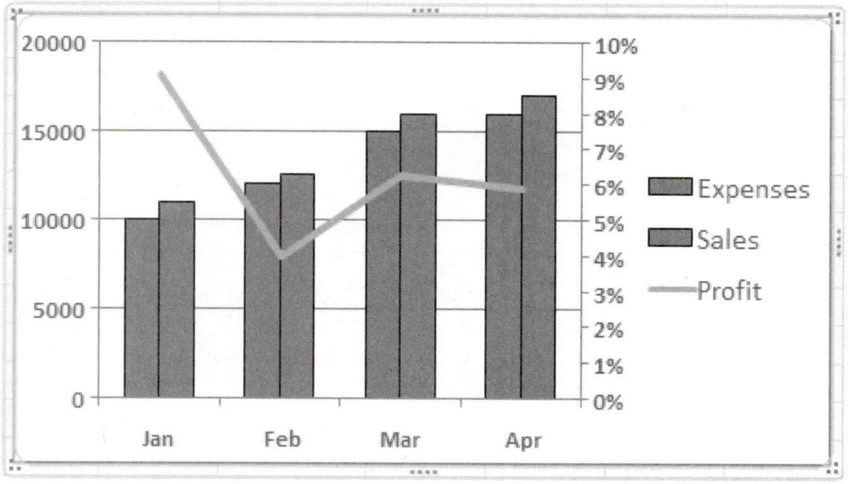

Exhibit 7-3: A sample column-line combination chart

To create a combination chart by changing the chart type of a data series:

1 Select the chart to display the Chart Tools tabs.
2 Activate the Format tab.
3 In the Current Selection group, in the Chart Area list, select the data series for which you want to change the chart type.
4 Activate the Design tab.
5 In the Type group, click Change Chart Type to open the Change Chart Type dialog box.
6 Select the chart type you want to apply to the selected data series.
7 Click OK.

To create a combination chart that uses a secondary value axis:

1 Select the chart.
2 Activate the Format tab.
3 In the Current Selection group, in the Chart Area list, select the data series that will use the secondary value axis.
4 In the Current Selection group, click Format Selection to open the Format Data Series dialog box.
5 Under Plot Series On, select Secondary Axis.
6 Click Close.

Do it!

B-1: Creating a combination chart

Here's how	Here's why
1 Activate the Combination worksheet	
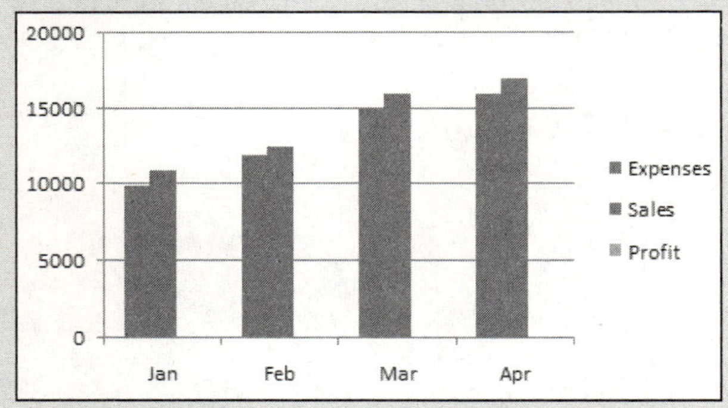	This sheet displays profit trends for four months. The category axis represents the months, and the value axis represents the sales. Profit columns are not visible because the Profit values are too small relative to the Expenses and Sales values.
2 Select the chart	

3 Activate the Format tab	If necessary.
In the Current Selection group, from the Chart Area list, select **Series "Profit"**	You'll create a secondary value axis to represent the Profit data series.
Click **Format Selection**	To open the Format Data Series dialog box. Series Options is selected by default.
4 Under Plot Series On, select **Secondary Axis**	To insert a secondary axis on the right side of the chart.
Click **Close**	To close the dialog box. The secondary axis appears on the right side of the chart. The chart columns for the Profit data series overlap the other columns.
5 Activate the Design tab	
6 In the Type group, click **Change Chart Type**	To display the Change Chart Type gallery. You'll assign a separate chart type to the Profit data series so that it will be represented as a line.
In the Chart Type list, choose **Line**	
7 In the Line gallery, click as shown	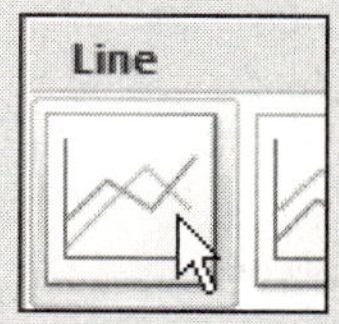 To select the first chart type under Line.
Click **OK**	To close the gallery and change the chart type for the Profit data series from column to line, as shown in Exhibit 5-2. Now it's easier to understand how profit percentages fluctuate with respect to expenses and sales.
8 Update the workbook	

Adding trendlines

Explanation

You can create a trendline in a chart to emphasize the pattern of change in your data. *Trendlines* are graphical representations of drifts or variations in a data series. Trendlines can highlight important variations and make your charts easier to understand, and they can facilitate forecasting and decision making.

To add a trendline to a chart:

1. Select the chart or data series to which you want to add a trendline.
2. Activate the Layout tab.
3. In the Analysis group, click Trendline.
4. From the menu, choose the type of trendline you want to apply.

Do it!

B-2: Creating a trendline

Here's how	Here's why
1 Activate the Trendline worksheet	

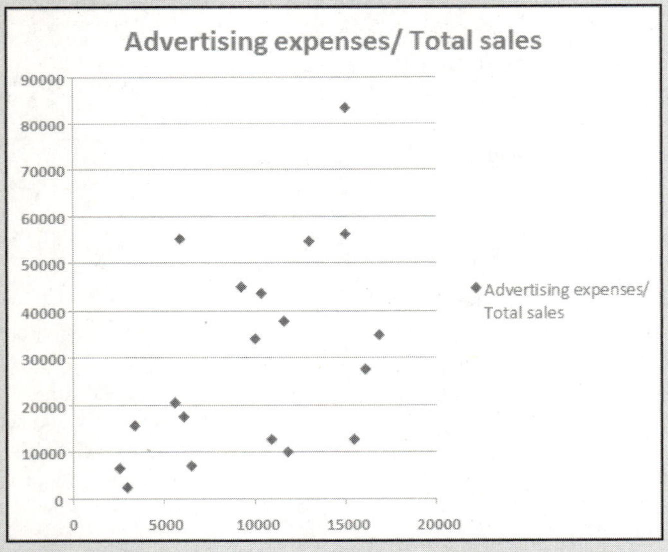

Here's how	Here's why
	This worksheet shows the advertising expenses and total sales for several years. In the chart, it's difficult to determine whether sales increased or decreased relative to changes in advertising expenses.
2 Select the chart	You'll create a trendline for the Advertising Expenses/Total Sales data series.
3 Activate the Layout tab	

4 In the Analysis group, click **Trendline** and choose **Linear Trendline**

To display the trendline on the chart. The trendline indicates that total sales increased as advertising expenses did.

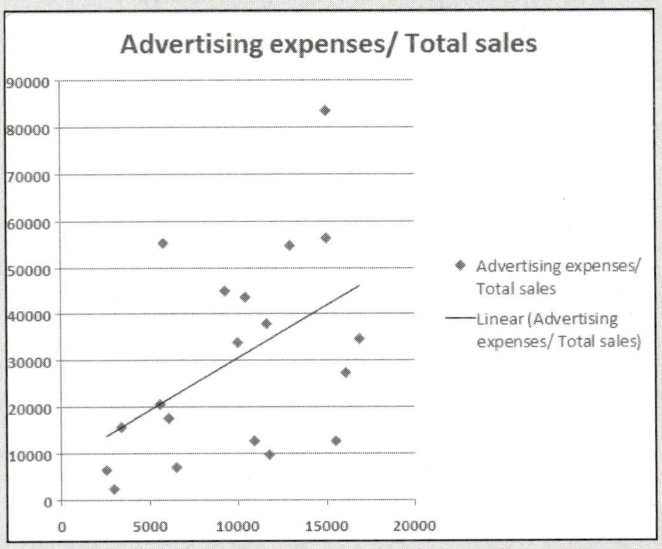

5 Update the workbook

Topic C: Graphic elements

This topic covers the following Microsoft Certified Application Specialist exam objective for Excel 2007.

#	Objective
4.4.1	**Insert and modify pictures from files** • Insert pictures • Modify pictures
4.4.3	**Insert and modify shapes**

Objects and shapes

Explanation

You can highlight a specific portion of a chart by adding graphic elements, such as text boxes, lines, and arrows. You can also format these elements to make them stand out or fit in better.

When you create or work with a shape, the Drawing Tools appear, adding a Format tab to the Ribbon.

Drawing objects

You can use the Shapes gallery to insert lines, arrows, shapes, and 3-D graphic objects in the chart area. To add a shape to a chart:

1. Select the chart and activate the Layout tab.
2. In the Insert group, click Shapes to display the Shapes gallery.
3. Select the desired shape and drag within the chart to create that shape.

You can also use the Insert group create drawing objects such as text boxes. To create a text box:

1. Activate the Layout tab.
2. In the Insert group, click Text Box. The pointer changes to a thin arrow pointing downward.
3. Point to where you want to place the text box, and drag to create the box.

Do it!

C-1: Adding graphic elements

Here's how	Here's why
1 Activate the Graphic sheet	This worksheet contains a chart of quarterly revenues and expenses. You'll add graphic elements to enhance the chart.
2 Select the chart	
Activate the Layout tab	
3 In the Insert group, click **Text Box**	The pointer changes to an arrow.
Drag to create a text box outside the chart	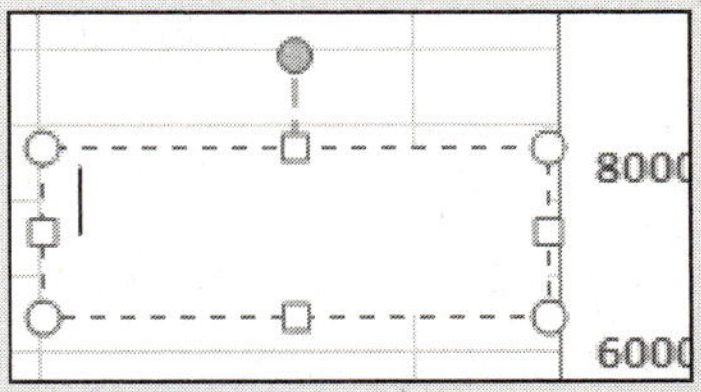 The Drawing Tools | Format tab appears on the Ribbon. You'll move and resize the box.
4 Move the text box as shown	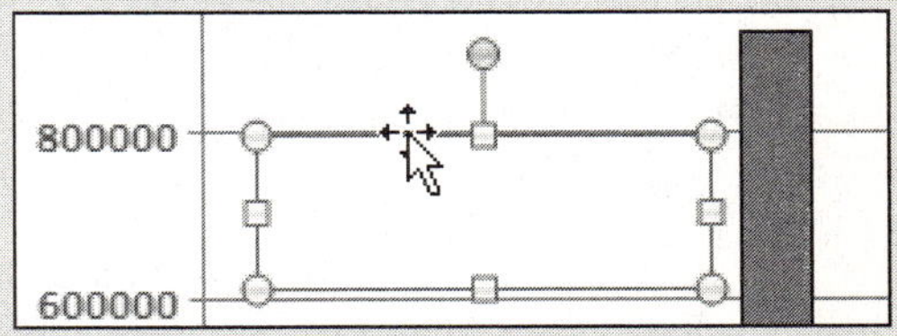 Drag it onto the chart.
5 Click in the text box and type **Sales hike**	You'll emphasize the steep rise in sales in the third quarter.
6 Resize the box to better fit the text	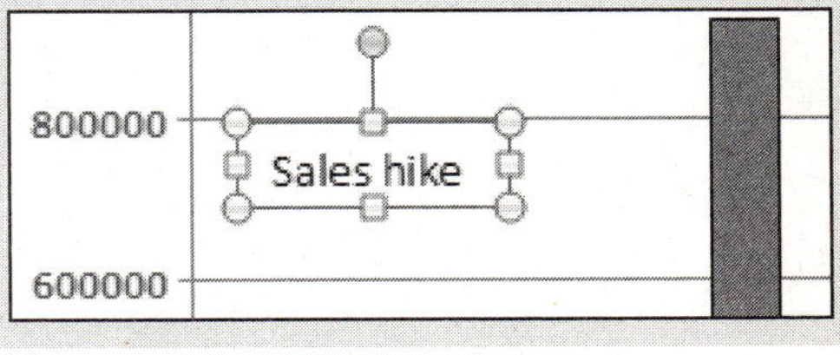

7 Select the text

Right-click the selected text

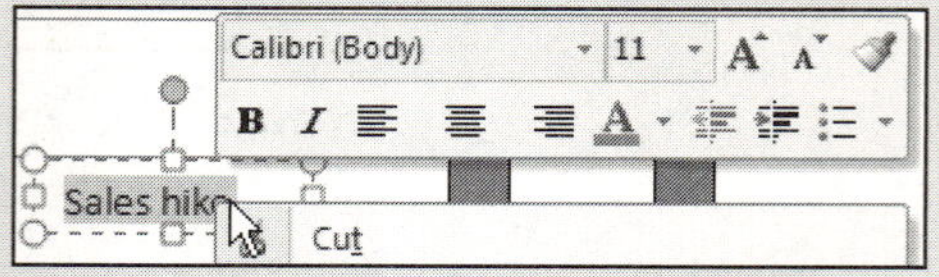

The Mini toolbar appears above the shortcut menu. You can choose different formatting styles, fonts, and font sizes here.

On the Mini toolbar, click 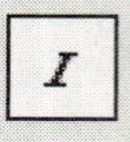

To apply the italic style to the selected text.

8 Activate the Format tab

Under Drawing Tools.

9 In the Insert Shapes group, click as shown

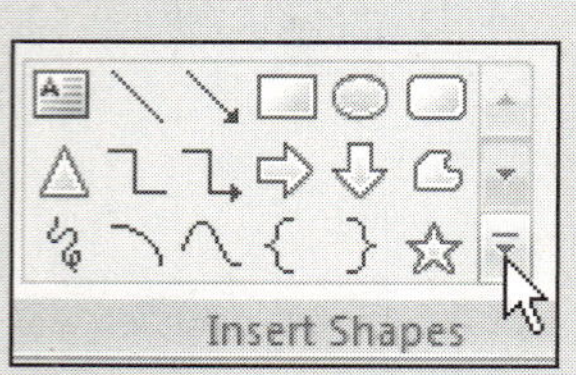

(The More button.) To display the Shapes gallery.

In the Shapes gallery, click as shown

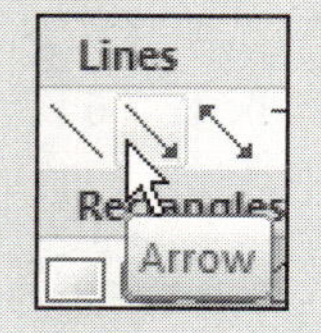

To select the Arrow line. The pointer takes the shape of a crosshair that you can use to draw an arrow.

10 Point to the upper-right corner of the text in the text box

The foot of the arrow will be here.

Drag as shown

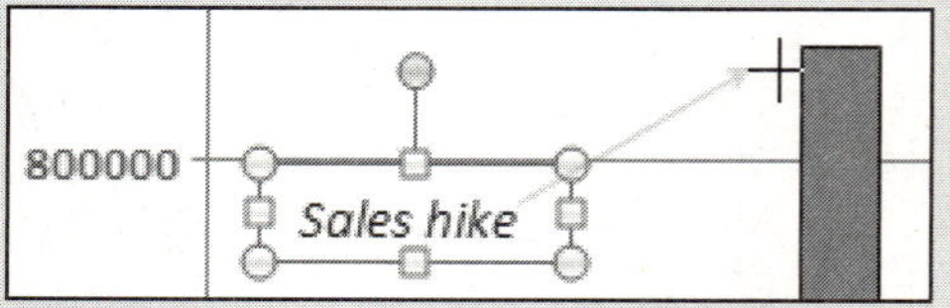

To create an arrow pointing from the text box to the tallest column of the chart. The text and the arrow emphasize the steep rise in sales.

Click outside the chart area

To observe the text box and arrow. You'll format the line in the next activity.

11 Update the workbook

Formatting graphic elements

Explanation

You can change the shape, size, or color of graphic elements. Here's how:

1. Double-click the graphic element you want to format.
2. On the Format tab, in the Shape Styles group, click either the Shape Fill, Shape Outline, or Shape Effects button to display a corresponding menu.
3. Choose an option from the menu. Some menu options display galleries, as shown in Exhibit 5-7.

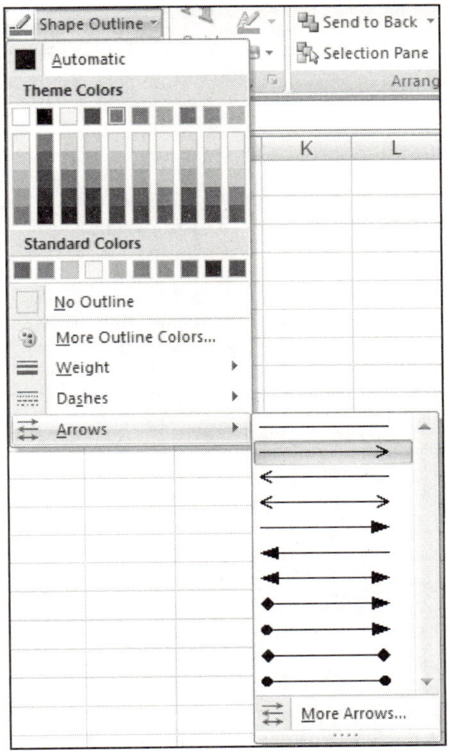

Exhibit 7-4: The Arrows gallery, accessed from the Shape Outline menu in the Shape Styles group

Do it!

C-2: Formatting a graphic element

Here's how	Here's why
1 Double-click the Sales hike arrow	To activate the Drawing Tools | Format tab.
2 In the Shape Styles group, click **Shape Effects**	To display a menu.
Choose **Shadow**	To display a gallery of shadow effects.
Point to the various effect options	To see a Live Preview of how the effects will look.
Click anywhere outside the Shadow gallery	To close it.
3 In the Shape Styles group, click **Shape Outline**	To display shape options.
Point to **Arrows**	To display the Arrows gallery. The current arrowhead style is highlighted.
Click as shown	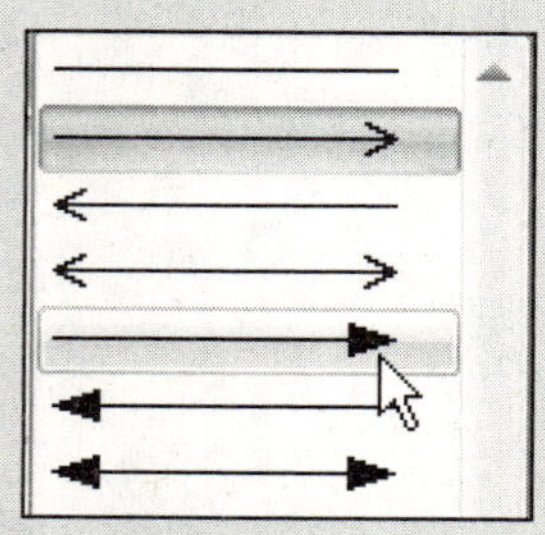 To apply Arrow Style 5 to the arrow in the chart.
4 Display the shape options again	Click Shape Outline.
Above Theme Colors, choose **Automatic**	To change the color of the arrow to black.
5 Update the workbook	

Working with pictures

Explanation

Including a picture on a worksheet can emphasize a specific point or add new information, as shown in Exhibit 5-2. You can insert pictures from the Clip Organizer or from files, or you can import pictures directly from a digital camera or scanner. After you have inserted a picture, you can move, resize, and delete it just as you would any other object.

To insert a picture from a file:

1. Select a cell in the worksheet.
2. Activate the Insert tab.
3. In the Illustrations group, click Picture to open the Insert Picture dialog box.
4. Open the folder that contains the picture.
5. Select the picture and click Insert.

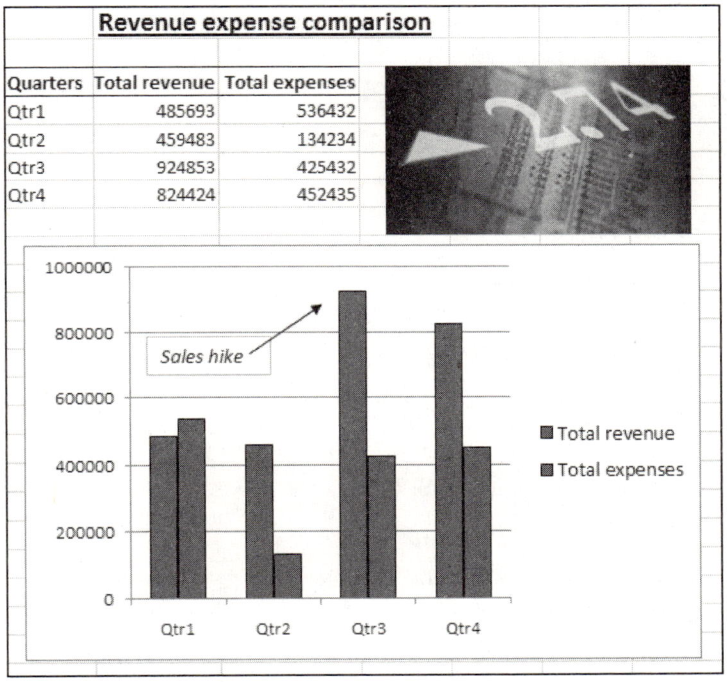

Exhibit 7-5: The Graphic worksheet with a picture inserted in it

When you insert or work with a picture, the Picture Tools appear, adding a Format tab to the Ribbon.

Resizing a picture

To resize a picture, you must first select it by clicking it. Then point to one of the sizing handles at the corners of the picture frame. The mouse pointer changes to a double-sided arrow. Drag the sizing handle to resize the picture.

To resize a picture proportionally, click and hold Shift before dragging the sizing handle. This forces the picture's height and width to resize at the same rate.

Modifying a picture

To move a picture, select it and drag it to a new location on the worksheet. If you want to move the picture to another worksheet or workbook, activate the Home tab. In the Clipboard group, click Cut. Then navigate to the destination worksheet or workbook and paste the picture.

You can use the buttons on the Format tab to rotate or crop a picture. Any picture in Excel can be cropped, except for an animated GIF.

You can also adjust a picture's brightness and contrast by using the Brightness and Contrast buttons on the Format tab.

Do it!

C-3: Adding a picture to a worksheet

Here's how	Here's why
1 Select E7	You'll insert a picture.
2 Activate the Insert tab	
3 In the Illustrations group, click **Picture**	To open the Insert Picture dialog box.
4 Navigate to the current unit folder	
Select **Profits**	
Click **Insert**	(You might need to scroll to view the picture.) To insert the picture. The Picture Tools | Format tab is active. The picture is large, so you'll crop and resize it.
5 In the Size group, click **Crop**	The pointer changes to an arrow with a cropping symbol.
6 Point to the upper-middle edge of the picture, and drag down as shown	 To crop the top portion of the picture. While the pointer is in Crop mode, dragging the corners or the middle edges crops the picture.
Click **Crop**	To exit Crop mode. The pointer changes.
7 Observe the Size group	The Height and Width boxes display the dimensions of the picture.

8	Press and hold SHIFT	
	While holding SHIFT, drag the lower-right handle up and to the left	To proportionally resize the picture.
	Release SHIFT	
9	Observe the Height and Width boxes	In the Size group. The boxes display the new size of the picture.
	Resize the picture proportionally to approximately 1.25" in height and 2.25" in width	Press and hold Shift, and drag a handle. Release Shift, and observe the dimensions in the Size group. Repeat as necessary.
10	Drag the picture to the right of the data	As shown in Exhibit 5-5.
11	In the Adjust group, click **Brightness**	To display the Brightness menu.
	Point to each value in the menu, while observing the picture	The Live Preview function displays the effect of changing the picture's brightness.
	Press ESC	To close the menu.
12	Click **Contrast**	The Contrast button is in the Picture Tools group.
	Observe the effect of different contrasts	Point to each value in the list.
	Close the Contrast menu	Press Esc.
	Deselect the picture	(Click any blank cell.) To close the Picture Tools | Format tab.
13	Update and close the workbook	

Unit summary: Advanced charting

Topic A In this topic, you learned how to adjust the **scale** of a chart. You also learned how to format **data points** by adding **data labels**. You learned that you can add data labels, such as the percentage value of a data point, to a chart. You also learned how to pull out a slice in a pie chart.

Topic B In this topic, you learned how to create a **combination chart** by using two value axes. You also learned how to add **trendlines**, which can be used to highlight the variations of data in a data series.

Topic C In this topic, you learned how to add and format **graphic elements**, which can be used to emphasize a specific point in a chart. You also learned how to add **pictures** to a worksheet.

Independent practice activity

In this activity, you'll change the values in the horizontal axis, change the maximum scale of the value axis, and add a text box and arrow. Then, you'll create a linear trendline.

1 Open Practice charts and save it as **My practice charts**.

2 Activate the Bonus sales worksheet, if necessary.

3 Change the category (horizontal) axis values to read **Q1**, **Q2**, **Q3**, **Q4**. (*Hint:* The values are in column A of the data.)

4 Change the maximum scale value of the value axis to **250**.

5 Add a text box to the worksheet, and enter **Lowest sales** in the box. Resize the box and the text to fit, apply the bold style, and then drag the text box onto the chart, as shown in Exhibit 7-6.

6 Add an arrow leading from the text box to the column showing the lowest sales. Apply Arrow Style 9 and the color black to the arrow.

7 Compare your chart with Exhibit 5-6.

8 Create a linear trendline for the data in the Trends worksheet.

9 Update and close the workbook.

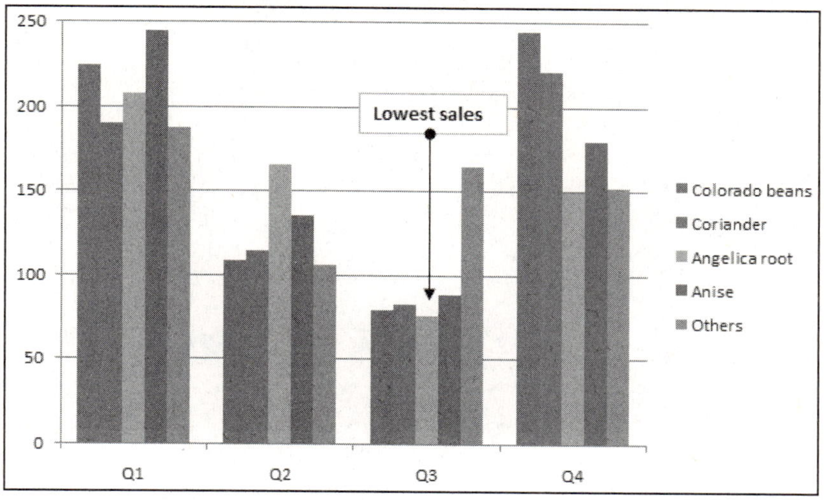

Exhibit 7-6: The chart after Step 6 of the independent practice activity

Review questions

1 How can you change the scale of a chart?

2 What is a leader line?

3 What is a combination chart?

4 What is a trendline?

5 List the steps you would use to insert a picture from a file.

Unit 8

Documenting and auditing

Unit time: 60 minutes

Complete this unit, and you'll know how to:

A Use auditing features to trace precedent and dependent cells, and trace errors.

B Add and edit comments for a cell and a worksheet.

C Protect a workbook or part of a worksheet from unauthorized access or unintentional changes.

D Share workbooks, merge versions of a workbook, track changes made by various users, remove personal data from a workbook, and mark a workbook as final.

Topic A: Auditing features

This topic covers the following Microsoft Certified Application Specialist exam objective for Excel 2007.

#	Objective
3.1.1	**Create formulas that use absolute and relative cell references**
	• Troubleshoot a formula

Tracing cell values

Explanation

You might want to identify the cells on which the value of a formula is based. Excel provides the Trace Precedents and Trace Dependents commands to point out such cells.

A *precedent cell* provides data to a specific cell. A *dependent cell* relies on the value of another cell. When you click the Trace Precedents and Trace Dependents buttons in the Formula Auditing group on the Formulas tab, Excel draws arrows showing precedent and dependent cells.

Do it!

A-1: Tracing precedent and dependent cells

Here's how	Here's why
1 Open Multi user	From the current unit folder.
Save the workbook as **My multi user**	In the current unit folder. The Monthly QOH worksheet contains a single month's quantity-on-hand totals for seven products.
2 Observe that the worksheet displays error values in some cells	These error values are indicated by the green triangles that appear in the upper-left corner of the cells.
3 Select C10	This cell contains the formula =D10/B10.
4 Activate the Formulas tab	
In the Formula Auditing group, click **Trace Precedents**	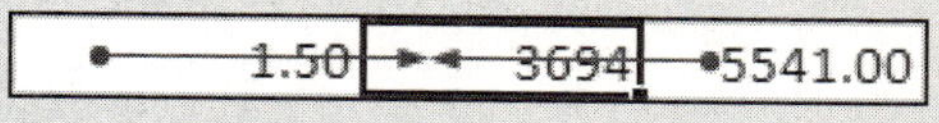 To trace the precedent cells of the selected cell. You can see two tracer arrows meeting at C10. These indicate that B10 and D10 provide values for the formula in C10 and are the precedent cells of C10.
5 In the Formula Auditing group, click **Remove Arrows**	To hide all tracer arrows.
6 Click **Trace Dependents**	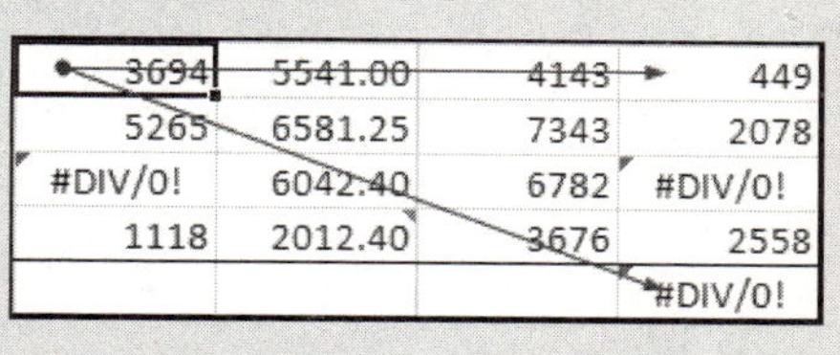 To trace the dependent cells of C10. Tracer arrows point from C10 to F10 and F14. The calculated values of F10 and F14 get their data from C10 and are the dependent cells of C10.
7 Hide the tracer arrows	Click Remove Arrows.
8 Update the workbook	

Tracing errors in a worksheet

Explanation

When Excel detects an error, it displays an error value (in the cell) and an Error Checking smart tag. You can click this smart tag to display a list of commands that can help you trace and correct the error. The Formula Auditing group on the Formulas tab also provides tools for this.

To trace an error, select the cell that contains the error; then, in the Formula Auditing group, click the down-arrow on the Error Checking button and choose Trace Error. You'll see tracer arrows pointing from the cell containing the error to other cells that provide values for the formula. An error in a cell might be caused by a reference to another cell that also contains an error. If so, a red arrow points to that cell. Blue arrows point from the cell where the error originates to the sources of that cell's formula.

Do it!

A-2: Tracing errors

Here's how	Here's why
1 Select F14	
2 In the Formula Auditing group, click the arrow beside Error Checking and choose **Trace Error**, as shown	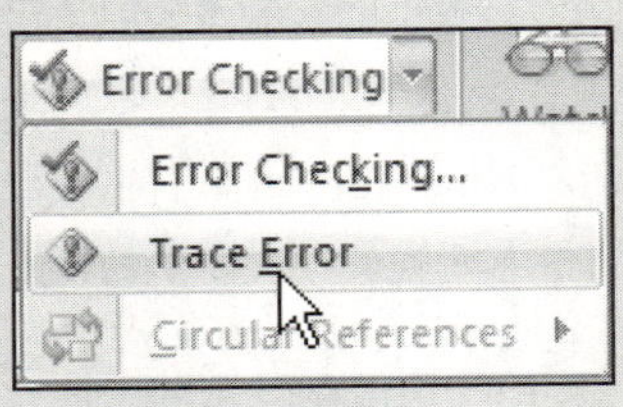 To display tracer arrows that show the source of the error produced by the formula in F14.
3 Observe the worksheet	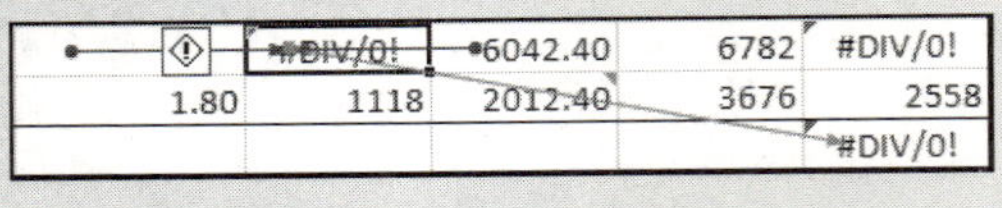 A red arrow points from C12 to F14. This arrow indicates that the cause of the error is the invalid value in C12. C12 gets its value from B12 and D12, as indicated by the blue arrows. B12 is empty, which causes the invalid value in C12.
4 In B12, enter **2**	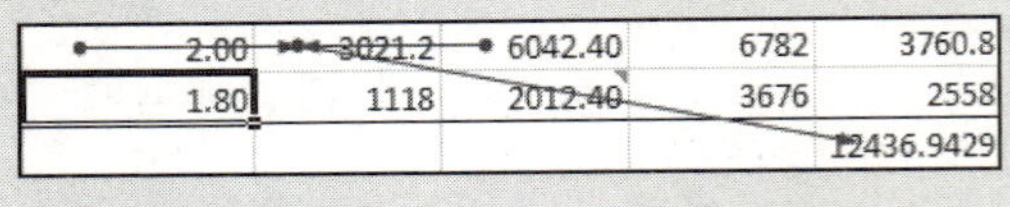 To correct the error values. The red arrow disappears, and valid numeric values replace the error values. The blue arrows indicate non-error conditions.
5 Hide the tracer arrows	
6 Update the workbook	

Topic B: Comments in cells and workbooks

This topic covers the following Microsoft Certified Application Specialist exam objective for Excel 2007.

#	Objective
5.1.2	**Insert, display, modify, and delete comments**
	• Insert comments
	• Edit comments
	• Delete comments
5.3.3	**Add keywords and other information to workbook properties**
	• Add keywords, author name, and other information to properties

Using and viewing comments

Explanation

A *comment* is a note or annotation that you can add to cells or workbooks to provide additional information. Adding comments to data makes your worksheet easier for other users to interpret. These comments do not alter the data in the cell. Comments in cells are denoted by small, red triangles, called *comment indicators*, in the upper-right corner of the cells.

To view a comment, point to the cell containing the comment indicator. To show all comments simultaneously, activate the Review tab. Then, in the Comments group, click Show All Comments. Click the button again to hide all comments.

Do it!

B-1: Viewing comments in a worksheet

Here's how	Here's why
1 Observe C9	 There is a red comment indicator in the upper-right corner of the cell.
2 Point to C9	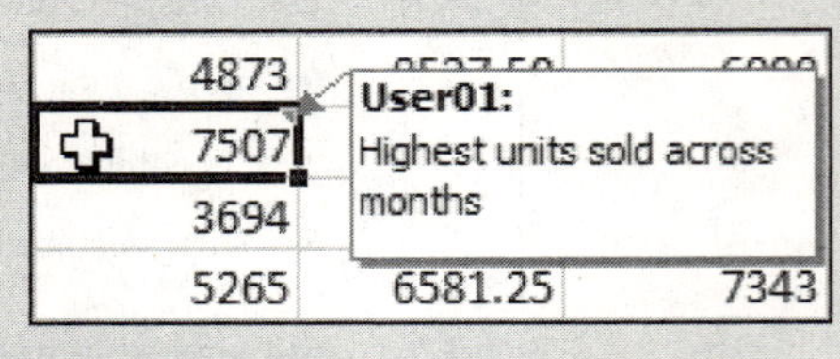 To display the associated comment. By default, cells always display comment indicators but do not display comments until you point to the cells.
Point to another cell	The comment disappears.
3 Activate the Review tab	
4 In the Comments group, click **Show All Comments**	To display all comments.

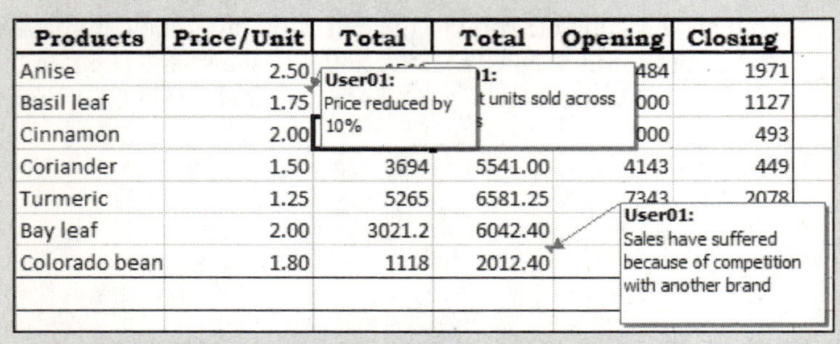

Here's how	Here's why
5 Click **Show All Comments**	To hide all the comments.

Adding and managing cell comments

Explanation

Comments can be added to cells and edited as needed.

To add a comment, select a cell and activate the Review tab. In the Comments group, click New Comment, and then enter text in the comment box that appears. After you've entered a comment, you might want to change it. To do so, select the cell containing the comment you want to edit. Click Edit Comment in the Comments group, or right-click the cell and choose Edit Comment. When you're finished making changes, click outside the comment box.

You can delete a comment by selecting the cell and clicking Delete in the Comments group, or by right-clicking the cell and choosing Delete Comment from the shortcut menu.

Comment display options

By using the Excel Options dialog box, you can customize the way comments and comment indicators appear. You can display only indicators, comments and indicators, or nothing at all. The default setting displays only the comment indicators, and displays a comment when you point to a cell. When you change the comment indicator settings, the new settings will be applied to all new workbooks.

Do it!

B-2: Adding a comment to a cell

Here's how	Here's why
1 Select E9	
2 In the Comments group, click **New Comment**	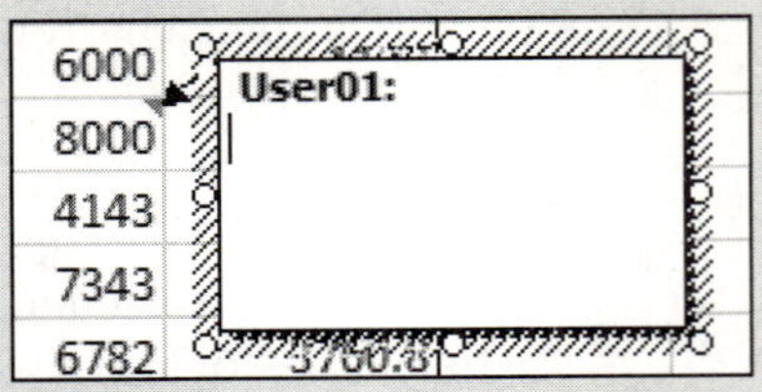 Your user name appears in the comment box. The red comment indicator appears in the upper-right corner of the cell.
Type **The decision to begin with a high opening stock worked.**	To add this information as a comment.
Click outside the comment box	The comment box disappears, but the cell displays the red comment indicator.
3 Point to E9	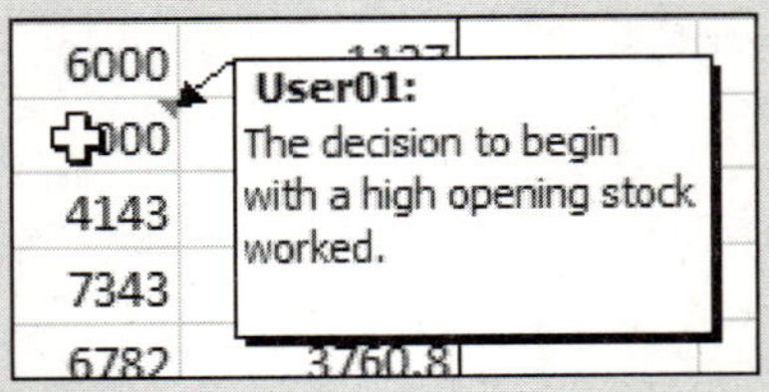 To view the comment you just added.
4 Click 	
Click **Excel Options**	To open the Excel Options dialog box. You'll view the display options for cell comments.
In the category list, select **Advanced**	
Under Display, observe the "For cells with comments, show" options	These options determine whether and how comments and their indicators are displayed. Changes made here affect this workbook and all new workbooks.
Click **Cancel**	To close the dialog box.

5 Select E9	You'll edit the comment you just added.
In the Comments group, click **Edit Comment**	To open the comment in Edit mode.
Change **The** to **Our**	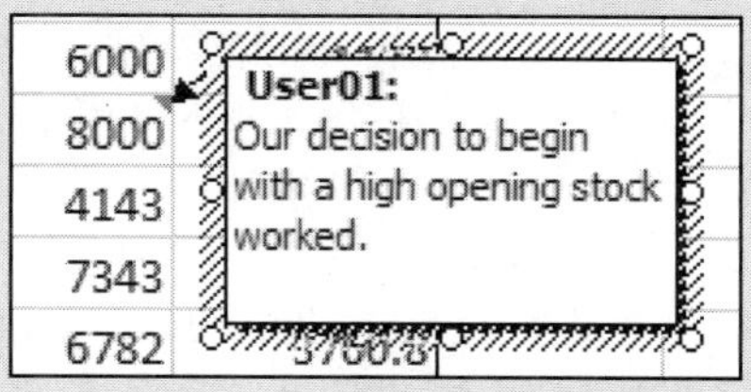
6 Click another cell	To close the comment and apply the edit.
View the comment	The comment reflects the change.
7 Right-click E9	To display a shortcut menu.
Choose **Delete Comment**	To delete the comment.
8 Update the workbook	

Adding workbook comments

Explanation

You can add a comment to a workbook by using the Document Information Panel, shown in Exhibit 6-1. This panel can also be used to enter workbook data, such as a descriptive title, a subject, an author name, a company name, and keywords.

To add comments and other information to an open workbook:

1. Click the Office Button and choose Prepare, Properties to open the Document Information Panel.
2. Enter descriptive information in the appropriate boxes.
3. Close the Document Information Panel.

Point to a workbook in Windows Explorer to display a ScreenTip that contains some of the workbook properties. This ScreenTip also appears when you point to a workbook in Excel's Open, Save, or Search dialog boxes.

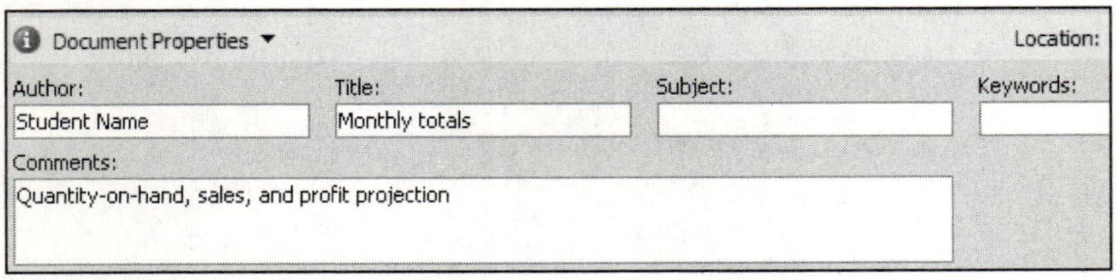

Exhibit 8-1: The Document Information Panel appears below the Ribbon

Do it!

B-3: Adding comments to a workbook

Here's how	Here's why
1 Click 	You'll add a comment to this workbook file.
Choose **Prepare**, **Properties**	To open the Document Information Panel below the Ribbon.
2 In the Author box, enter your name	By default, the Author box is populated with the user name from your PC. Change it to your own name.
In the Title box, enter **Monthly Totals**	
3 In the Comments box, enter **Quantity-on-hand, sales, and profit projection**	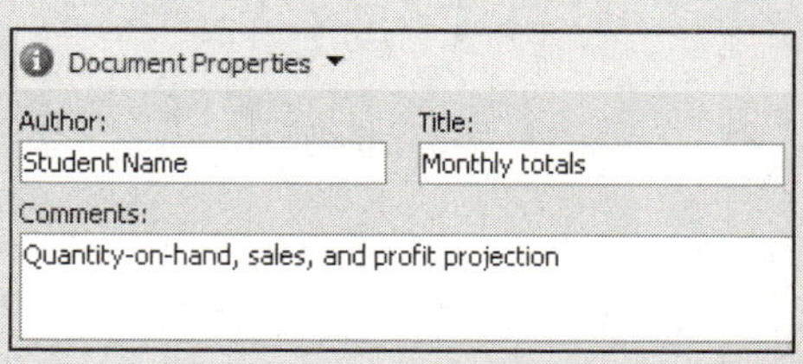 To enter additional information about the workbook content.
Close the Document Information Panel	Click the "X" in the top-right corner of the panel.
4 Update the workbook	To save these changes.
5 Display the Open dialog box	
Point to **My multi user**	 A ScreenTip appears with file information, including comments and some of the other information you added in the Document Information Panel. Note that the Company name is not included.
Click **Cancel**	To close the dialog box.
6 Update the workbook	

Topic C: Protection

This topic covers the following Microsoft Certified Application Specialist exam objectives for Excel 2007.

#	Objective
5.2.1	**Protect workbooks and worksheets** • Prevent changes to worksheets • Allow users to edit ranges • Require passwords to open workbooks
5.3.2	**Restrict permissions to a workbook** • Enable a specific user to change a workbook by using Information Rights Management (IRM).
5.3.4	**Add digital signatures**

Preventing unauthorized changes

Explanation

By protecting a worksheet, you can prevent unauthorized users from modifying it. You can protect an entire worksheet or protect only a part of it, permitting users to alter the other parts.

Applying password protection to a worksheet

You might need to prevent the data in a worksheet from being altered accidentally or accessed by unauthorized users. You can use the Protect Sheet dialog box to password-protect a worksheet.

To password-protect a worksheet:

1. Activate the Review tab.
2. In the Changes group, click Protect Sheet to open the Protect Sheet dialog box, shown in Exhibit 6-3.
3. Check the options you want.
4. Type a password and click OK. The Confirm Password dialog box appears.
5. In the "Reenter password to proceed" box, type the same password.
6. Click OK to close both the password confirmation box and the dialog box.

Before entering data into a password-protected sheet, you must unprotect it. To do so, click Unprotect Sheet in the Changes group; this opens the Unprotect Sheet dialog box. In the Password box, enter the password, and then click OK.

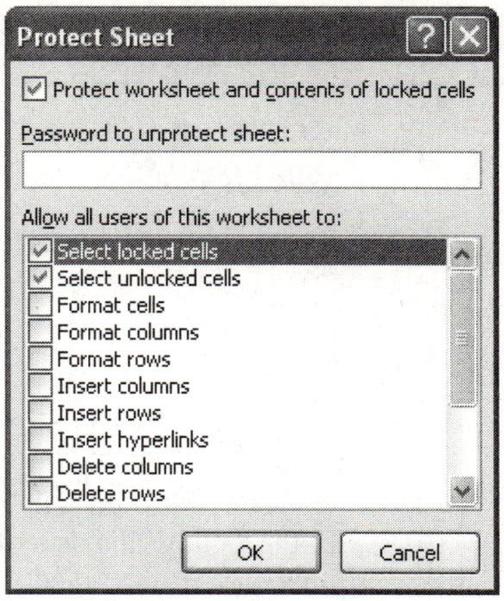

Exhibit 8-2: The Protect Sheet dialog box

Protecting a workbook

Similarly, to protect a workbook, click Protect Workbook in the Changes group. In the Protect Workbook dialog box that appears, you can protect a workbook's structure and windows. By selecting Structure, you protect a workbook from being moved, deleted, hidden, unhidden, or renamed, and new worksheets can't be inserted. By selecting Windows, you ensure that a workbook's windows are the same size and position each time the workbook is opened. To prevent other users from removing workbook protection, you can set a password. After specifying settings in the Protect Workbook dialog box, click OK.

Do it!

C-1: Password-protecting a worksheet

Here's how	Here's why
1 Activate the Review tab	If necessary.
2 In the Changes group, click **Protect Sheet**	 To open the Protect Sheet dialog box, shown in Exhibit 6-2. The option "Protect worksheet and contents of locked cells" is checked by default. In the "Allow all users of this worksheet to" list, only "Select locked cells" and "Select unlocked cells" are checked.
In the "Password to unprotect sheet" box, enter **User01**	The entry in this field is masked by a row of dots. This prevents it from being read by someone looking over your shoulder. This masking occurs in all fields in which you enter a password.
Click **OK**	To open the Confirm Password dialog box.
3 In the "Reenter password to proceed" box, enter **User01**	
Click **OK**	To confirm the password you entered. Both this box and the Protect Sheet dialog box close.
4 Enter a new value in B11	A message box appears, stating that the cell is protected, and as a result, you cannot enter a value or change the worksheet.
Click **OK**	To close the message box.
5 Click **Unprotect Sheet**	(In the Changes group.) A dialog box appears, prompting you for the password.
In the Password box, enter **User01**	
Click **OK**	
6 In B11, enter **1.5**	You can now enter a value in the worksheet.
7 Update the workbook	

Protecting parts of a worksheet

Explanation

When you password-protect an entire worksheet, all cells in that worksheet are locked by default. This means that users cannot change any of the cells. To permit users to change some specific cells, you must unlock the cells manually before protecting the rest of the worksheet. Users can then change data in only the unlocked cells. The rest of the worksheet remains protected. One typical application of this is to unlock the cells containing raw values to permit data entry, and lock the cells containing formulas.

To protect only a part of a worksheet:

1. Select the range of cells that you want users to be able to modify.
2. Right-click and choose Format Cells to open the Format Cells dialog box.
3. Activate the Protection tab.
4. Clear the Locked check box and click OK.
5. Protect the worksheet. You don't necessarily need to use a password.

Do it!

C-2: Protecting part of a worksheet by unlocking cells

Here's how	Here's why
1 Select B7:B13	You'll keep these cells unlocked while protecting the rest of the worksheet.
2 Right-click and choose **Format Cells...**	To open the Format Cells dialog box.
3 Activate the Protection tab	
Clear **Locked**	
Click **OK**	To close the dialog box and unlock the selected range of cells.
4 Protect the sheet without entering a password	(In the Changes group, click Protect Sheet.) You'll protect the sheet, but users will be able to modify the unlocked cells in the range B7:B13.
Click **OK**	Because you did not enter a password, any user can unprotect the worksheet by using the Unprotect Sheet dialog box.
5 In B11, enter **2.5**	You can enter the value in the unlocked cell.
6 In D10, enter a value	A message box appears, stating that the cell is protected, and as a result, you cannot enter a value or change the worksheet.
Click **OK**	
7 Click **Unprotect Sheet**	
Update the workbook	

Restricting permissions to workbooks

Explanation

You can specify who may access a workbook by restricting *permissions*. Permissions refer to certain rules associated with a file that is shared on a network. For example, you might want to specify that other individuals can read the workbook but not edit it. This prevents unauthorized changes in the data. To implement permissions, Microsoft Office 2007 utilizes the Information Rights Management technology.

Information Rights Management

In order to use Information Rights Management to restrict permissions to a workbook, your computer needs the Windows Rights Management Services (RMS) Client installed. Typically, RMS components are installed and managed by an RMS administrator. Once these services are enabled, you can use them to restrict permissions to a workbook.

Permission levels for IRM are as follows:

Level	Description
Read	Allows users to read the workbook, but not change, print, or copy it.
Change	Allows users to read, edit, and save changes to a workbook, but not print it
Full Control	Allows users full authority to read, change, copy, and print, as well as restrict permissions for other users.

To restrict permissions with IRM, click the Office Button and choose Prepare, Restrict Permission, Restricted Access. This opens the Permission dialog box, as shown in Exhibit 8-3. In the Read and Change boxes, enter the e-mail addresses of the individuals to whom you want to grant permissions. When you're done, click OK.

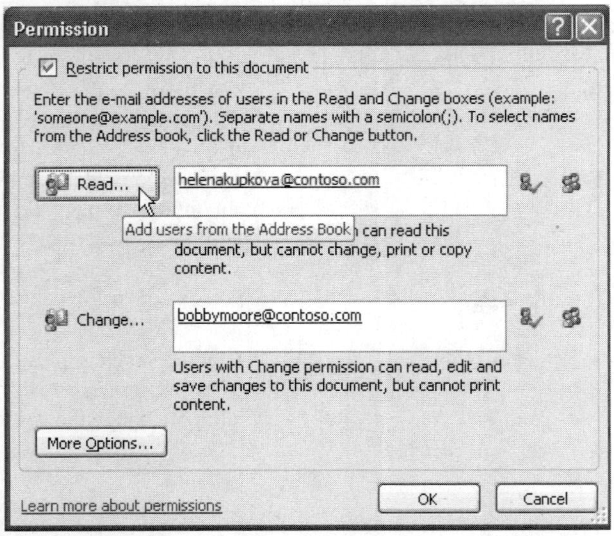

Exhibit 8-3: The Permission dialog box

Do it!

C-3: Restricting permissions to a workbook

Questions and answers

1 Why might you want to restrict permissions to a workbook?

2 What technology does Microsoft Office 2007 use to implement permissions?

3 Describe the difference between the Read and Change permission levels.

4 In order to use the IRM service, you must first have what installed on your computer?

Protecting worksheets by using digital signatures

Explanation

When you send worksheets or other documents over the Internet, there is a chance that someone might access and alter them. To protect your documents from unauthorized access, you can use digital signatures. A *digital signature* is an electronic security stamp that is used to authenticate files that are sent over the Internet. To use a digital signature, you need to install a *digital certificate*, which is an attachment that guarantees security for a file.

To obtain a digital certificate, you should submit an application to a commercial certification authority, such as VeriSign Inc. You can also obtain a digital certificate from your internal security administrator or from an Information Technology professional. It's also possible to create your own digital certificates, called *self-signed projects*. However, self-signed projects might not be legally valid because they are not sanctioned by any legal authority.

When you receive a digital certificate, included are instructions on how to install it on your computer. After installing the certificate, you can use it to sign the files that you send through the Internet.

To add a digital signature:

1 Save the workbook.
2 Click the Office Button and choose Prepare, Add a Digital Signature to open the Signature dialog box.
3 Complete the "Purpose for signing this document" box and click Sign.

Do it!

C-4: Discussing digital signatures

Questions and answers

1 What is a digital signature?

2 Why do you need a digital signature?

3 What is a digital certificate?

4 If you create your own digital certificate, is it legally valid?

Topic D: Workgroup collaboration

This topic covers the following Microsoft Certified Application Specialist exam objectives for Excel 2007.

#	Objective
5.1.1	**Insert, display, modify, and resolve tracked changes** • Begin tracking changes • Resolve tracked changes
5.2.2	**Enable workbooks to be changed by multiple users** • Share a workbook by using the Share Workbook command
5.3.1	**Remove private and other inappropriate data from workbooks** • Determine when to use the Document Inspector
5.3.5	**Mark workbooks as final** • Certify and protect content from changes by marking as final

Sharing workbooks

Explanation

Sharing a workbook makes it possible for several co-workers to collaborate on the same set of data. For example, several sales managers could enter their respective regional sales figures in the same workbook, eliminating the need to collect and consolidate the data manually.

To share a workbook:

1. Open the workbook that you want to share.
2. Activate the Review tab.
3. In the Changes group, click Share Workbook to open the Share Workbook dialog box. Activate the Editing tab.
4. Check "Allow changes by more than one user at the same time" and click OK.
5. Save the workbook in a location where other users can access it

Modifying a shared workbook

To edit a shared workbook, open it from its network location. Then make changes in the workbook as usual.

When modifying a shared workbook, you won't be able to change the following elements: merged cells, conditional formats, data validation, charts, pictures, objects (including drawing objects), hyperlinks, scenarios, outlines, subtotals, data tables, PivotTable reports, workbook and worksheet protection, and macros.

Do it!

D-1: Sharing a workbook

Here's how	Here's why
1 Activate the Review tab	If necessary.
In the Changes group, click **Share Workbook**	 To open the Share Workbook dialog box. By default, the Editing tab is active.
2 Check **Allow changes by more than one user at the same time**	
Click **OK**	A message box appears, warning you that this action will save the workbook.
Click **OK**	The name of the workbook changes to "My multi user [Shared]."

Merging workbooks

Explanation

You might need to share a workbook among users who cannot access the same file simultaneously. You can do this by distributing copies of the shared workbook, permitting users to change their copies, and then merge those copies into a single workbook.

To begin, share the workbook as described previously. Then make copies of the workbook and distribute them to the users.

You can control how a workbook is shared by using the Advanced tab in the Share Workbook dialog box, shown in Exhibit 6-3. For example, under Update changes, you can select "When file is saved" to see the changes made by other users each time you save the workbook. You can also set the interval at which changes will be shown automatically.

After the users have changed their copies of the workbook, you can merge the copies into a single workbook. To merge workbooks:

1. Open the Excel Options dialog box.
2. Select Customize, and add Compare and Merge Workbooks to the Quick Access toolbar.
3. On the Quick Access toolbar, click the Compare and Merge Workbooks button to open the Select Files to Merge Into Current Workbook dialog box.
4. Select the copies of the workbook that contain changes you want to merge.
5. Click OK.

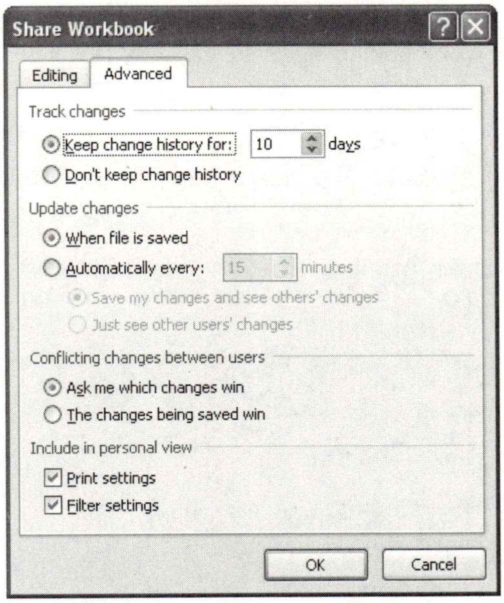

Exhibit 8-4: The Advanced tab in the Share Workbook dialog box

Do it!

D-2: Merging workbooks

Here's how	Here's why
1 Open the Excel Options dialog box	(Click the Office Button and click Excel Options.) You'll make a merging command available by adding it to the Quick Access toolbar.
From the category list, select **Customize**	To display the Customize the Quick Access Toolbar page.
Under "Customize Quick Access toolbar," verify that "For all documents (default)" is selected	You'll make these changes effective for all workbooks, not just the one that's open.
2 Under Choose commands from, select **All commands**	To display all available commands.
Select **Compare and Merge Workbooks...**	Scroll down. Commands are in alphabetical order.
Click **Add**	To add the Compare and Merge Workbooks command to the Quick Access toolbar.
Click **OK**	To save the changes and close the Excel Options dialog box.
3 Open the Share Workbook dialog box	In the Changes group, click Share Workbook.
Activate the Advanced tab	Under Track changes, "Keep change history for" is selected. You'll maintain a history of changes made by various users.
Under Track changes, edit the days box to read **10**	As shown in Exhibit 6-1. This setting will permit users to track the change history for 10 days.
Click **OK**	
4 Activate the Sales report worksheet	
Update the workbook	
5 Save the workbook as **Copy of my multi user**	You'll merge this workbook with another one.
6 Select A4:E4	You'll change the format of the data, and see the changes being applied to the workbook My multi user.
Right-click the selection	The Mini toolbar appears.

7	On the Mini toolbar, click as shown	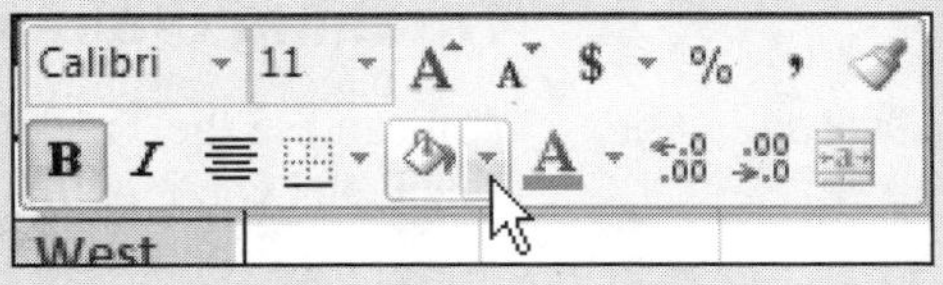 To display the Fill Color gallery.
	Apply light blue shading to the selection	
8	Apply light green shading to A5:A14	Right-click, and select a color by using the Fill Color button on the Mini toolbar.
9	Apply another color of shading to A15:E15	
	Deselect the range	
	Update and close the workbook	
10	Open My multi user	
	Save the workbook as **Copy2 of my multi user**	You'll consolidate the changes by merging the two copies of the workbook with the original workbook.
11	Verify that Sales report is the active worksheet	
	In B5, enter **840**	
	Update and close the workbook	
12	Open My multi user	
13	On the Quick Access toolbar, click 	(The Compare and Merge Workbooks icon.) You'll update the current workbook with the changes you made in "Copy of my multi user" and "Copy2 of my multi user." The Select Files to Merge Into Current Workbook dialog box opens.
	Select **Copy of my multi user**	In the current unit folder.
	Press CTRL and select **Copy2 of my multi user**	
	Click **OK**	
14	Observe the Sales report sheet	The format of the data changes to what you had applied in "Copy of my multi user." The ranges now have the shading you applied, and the value in B5 changed to $840.
15	Update the workbook	

Tracking changes

Explanation

You can use the Track Changes feature to examine the changes made in a workbook. This helps you identify who made changes, when they were made, what the original values were, and what the new values are. If your workbook is not shared, Excel makes the workbook shared automatically when you turn on the Track Changes feature.

To highlight changes:

1. Activate the Review tab.
2. In the Changes group, click Track Changes and choose Highlight Changes to open the Highlight Changes dialog box.
3. If the workbook is not shared, check "Track changes while editing." If the workbook is shared, this option will be checked by default.
4. Specify how you want the changes to be tracked:
   - If you want to view changes based on when they were made—for example, after a specific date—check When and select the necessary setting from the list.
   - If you want to view the changes made by a specific user, check Who and select Everyone or Everyone but Me from the list.
   - If you want to view the changes made in a specific range, check Where and enter the range.
5. Click OK.

To review workbook changes and accept or reject them:

1. Activate the Review tab.
2. In the Changes group, click Track Changes and choose Accept/Reject Changes. You'll be prompted to save the workbook.
3. Click OK to save the workbook. The Select Changes to Accept or Reject dialog box appears.
4. If you want to view changes based on when they were made, check When and select a time period.
5. Click OK to open the Accept or Reject Changes dialog box. At the same time, a cell that contains a changed value will be highlighted. The dialog box displays information about each change, including the name of the person who made the change, the date and time it was made, and other changes that will occur if you accept or reject the suggested change. You can scroll down to view the rest of the contents.
6. Click Accept to accept the change, or click Reject to restore the original value. The next cell with a changed value will be highlighted.

Do it!

D-3: Tracking changes in a workbook

Here's how	Here's why
1 Activate the Profit projection sheet	
2 In B7, enter **60000**	This is the new total sales value for Qtr 1.
3 Activate the Review tab	If necessary.
In the Changes group, click **Track Changes** and choose **Highlight Changes...**	To open the Highlight Changes dialog box. By default, "Since I last saved" is entered in the When box, and "Everyone" is entered in the Who box.
Click **OK**	
4 Point to B7	A comment appears, stating that the value in B7 has changed from $50,000.00 to $60,000.00. The comment includes the name of the user who made the change and the date and time it was made.
5 Click **Track Changes** and choose **Accept/Reject Changes**	(In the Changes group.) A message box appears, stating that the workbook will be saved.
Click **OK**	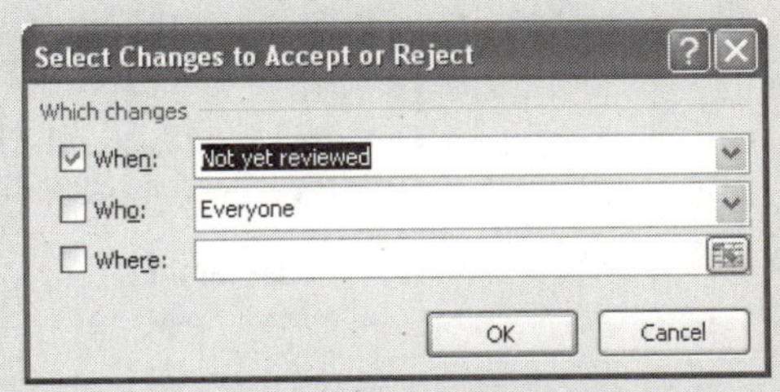 To open the Select Changes to Accept or Reject dialog box. By default, the When box is checked.
Click **OK**	To open the Accept or Reject Changes dialog box, which shows the original and changed values for B5.
6 Click **Accept**	To accept the change.
7 Update the workbook	

Preparing workbooks for distribution

Explanation

Before sharing a workbook via e-mail, print, or the Web, you might want to be sure that any personal or hidden information contained in the workbook is removed. Hidden and personal details in a workbook could reveal information about you or your organization that you want to keep private.

Some types of hidden or personal information that might be found in a workbook include:

- Hidden rows, columns, or worksheets
- Document properties, such as author, or workbook comments
- Cell comments and revision marks from tracked changes

To help you find and remove hidden or private information in a workbook, Excel provides the Document Inspector, shown in Exhibit 8-5.

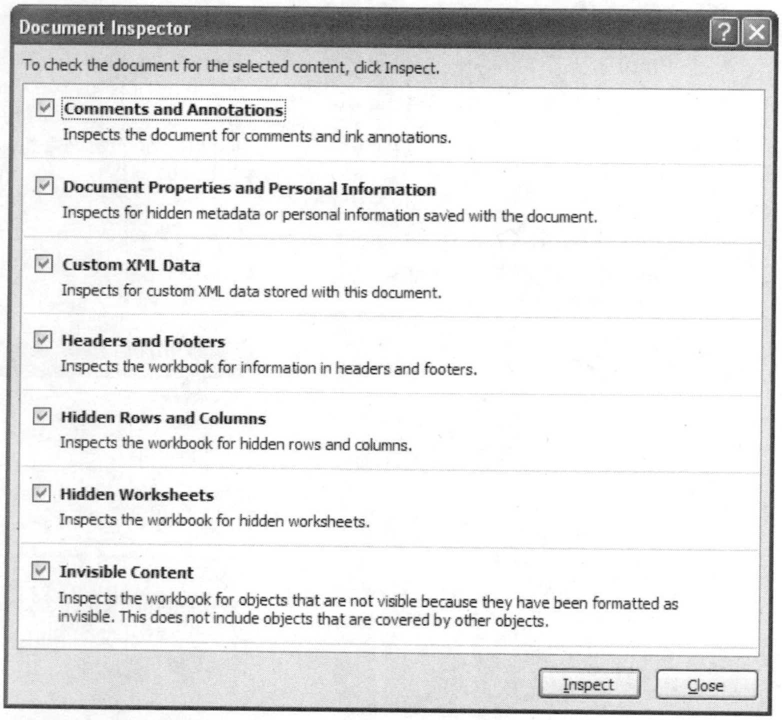

Exhibit 8-5: The Document Inspector

Before using the Document Inspector, first save a copy of the file you want to examine, and unshare the workbook. The Document Inspector might remove data that isn't always possible to restore later if needed, and it cannot remove data from a shared workbook.

To use the Document Inspector:

1. Click the Office Button and choose Prepare, Inspect Document to open the Document Inspector.
2. Check the items you want the Document Inspector to search for.
3. Click Inspect.
4. If you want to remove the hidden or private content found, click Remove All.
5. Click Close.

Do it!

D-4: Using the Document Inspector

Here's how	Here's why
1 Save the workbook as **Copy3 of My multi user**	Even though you're making a copy of My multi-user, the copy is still shared. You have to unshare the workbook before using the Document Inspector.
2 In the Changes group, click **Share Workbook**	To open the Share Workbook dialog box.
On the Editing tab, uncheck **Allow changes by more than one user at the same time**	
Click **OK**	To close the box and unshare the workbook. A message box appears.
Click **Yes**	To close the message box.
3 Click 	
Choose **Prepare**, **Inspect Document**	To open the Document Inspector dialog box. All content is checked by default.
4 Click **Inspect**	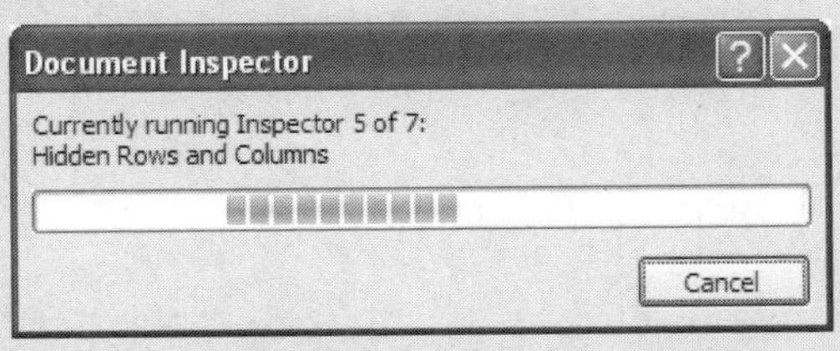 A window appears indicating the Inspector's progress.
5 Observe the screen	

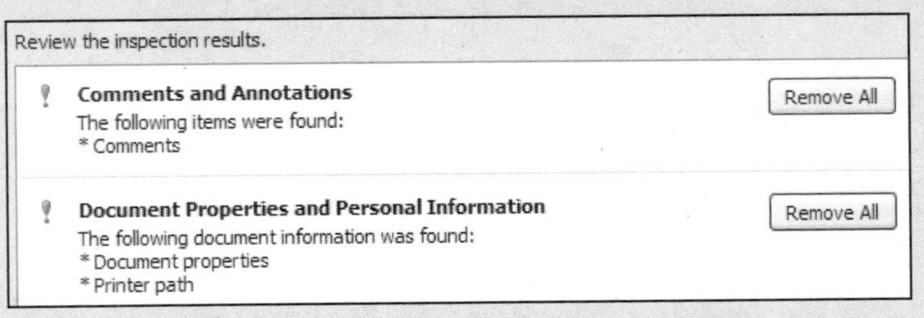

The Inspector found comments, document information, and the printer path.

6 To the right of Comments and Annotations, click **Remove All**	To remove all comments from the workbook.
Remove the document properties and personal information found	Click Remove All.
Click **Close**	To close the Document Inspector.
7 Update the workbook	

Finalizing workbooks

Explanation

When you have finished making changes and removing private data from a workbook, you can use the Mark as Final command to mark the workbook as read-only and prevent any further changes in it.

To mark a workbook as final, click the Office Button and choose Prepare, Mark as Final. A message box appears, indicating that the workbook will be marked as final and then saved. Click OK. You will then see a message box with information about the status of the document, as shown in Exhibit 8-6.

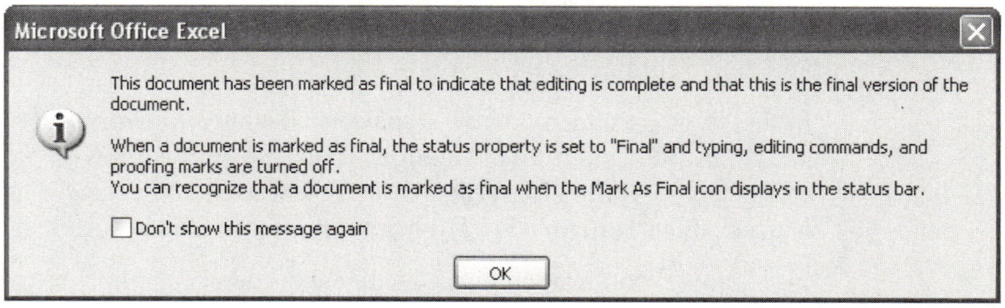

Exhibit 8-6: The message box that appears after you mark a workbook as final

Do it!

D-5: Marking a workbook as final

Here's how	Here's why
1 Click 	
2 Choose **Prepare**, **Mark as Final**	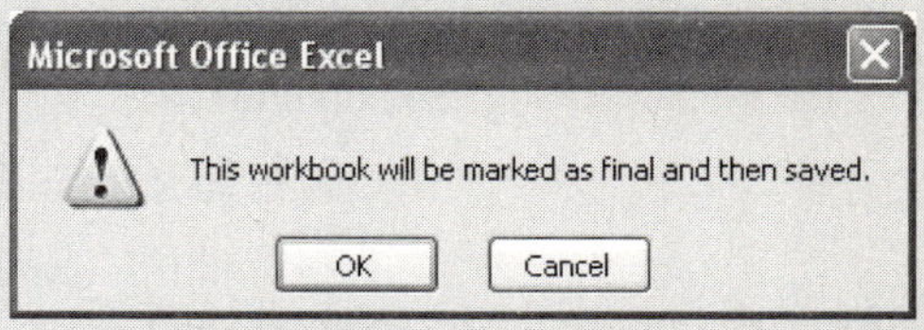 A message box appears.
3 Click **OK**	A message box appears with information about the status of the workbook.
4 Observe the status bar	 The Marked as Final icon appears.
5 In B8, enter 30000	Nothing happens because the workbook will no longer allow any changes.
Close the workbook	It isn't necessary to update it.

Unit summary: Documenting and auditing

Topic A In this topic, you learned how to use the **Formula Auditing** group to **trace precedent** and **dependent cells** and to view the relationships between formulas in a worksheet. You learned that a precedent cell provides a value to another cell, and a dependent cell depends on another cell for a value. You also learned how to **trace errors**.

Topic B In this topic, you learned how to add **comments** to cells. You learned that a comment is used to provide additional information about data. You also learned how to display one comment at a time and how to display all comments together. In addition, you learned how to change the **comment indicator** settings. Finally, you learned how to add, edit, and delete comments for a workbook.

Topic C In this topic, you learned how to **password-protect** a worksheet to prevent unauthorized users from changing it. You also learned how to protect only a part of a worksheet by **unlocking cells** that you want users to be able to modify. You also learned about **Information Rights Management** and **digital signatures**.

Topic D In this topic, you learned how to **share** workbooks and how to **merge** copies of shared workbooks that various users have changed. You learned that sharing a workbook permits multiple users to work on it at the same time. You also learned how to **track changes** in a workbook and accept or reject tracked changes. Finally, you learned how to use the **Document Inspector** to find and remove private data before distributing a workbook, and how to mark a workbook as final.

Independent practice activity

In this activity, you'll add a comment to a cell and trace errors, precedent cells, and dependent cells. Then you'll unlock a range and protect the rest of the worksheet. Next, you'll share the workbook and merge changes from several workbooks. Finally, you'll track changes.

1. Open Practice multi user and save it as **My practice multi user**.
2. In B5, add this comment: **Constantly increasing fixed costs kept the profit percentage low.**
3. Trace the cells causing the error value in F7.
4. Trace the precedent and dependent cells of D5.
5. Compare your result with Exhibit 6-2.
6. Remove all arrows.
7. Unlock B4:C9; then protect the worksheet using **password** as a password.
8. Unprotect the worksheet.
9. Update the workbook.
10. Share the workbook, allowing changes by more than one user at a time.
11. Save the workbook as **Copy of my practice multi user**. Then, in the Bonus sales analysis sheet, apply a new colored shading to A6:E6, and a different color shading to A8:E22. When you're done, update the workbook and close it.
12. Open My practice multi user.
13. Merge My practice multi user with Copy of my practice multi user, and observe the changes in the Bonus sales analysis sheet.

14 In the Bonus sales report sheet, in A3, enter **Name**. In E5, enter **5000**. Track the changes you made. Restore the original value in A3. Accept the change in E5.

15 Unshare the workbook.

16 Run the Document Inspector to search for inappropriate or private data. Remove all instances found.

17 Mark the workbook as final.

18 Close the workbook.

	A	B	C	D	E	F
1						
2	**Regional Profits**					
3	Region	Fixed cost	Variable cost	Total cost	Total revenue	%Profit
4	North	60000	55000	115000	135000	15%
5	South	80000	75000	155000	160000	3%
6	East	90000	80000	170000	182000	7%
7	Central	107500	88000	195500		#DIV/0!
8	West	109000	90000	199000	225000	12%
9	HQ	110000	96000	206000	236000	13%

Exhibit 8-7: The worksheet after Step 5

Review questions

1 What are precedent and dependent cells? How can you identify them in a worksheet?

2 When you click the Trace Error button, you'll see red and/or blue tracer arrows pointing from the cell containing the error to other cells. What do the red and blue arrows mean?

3 List the steps you would use to password-protect a worksheet.

4 If you choose to protect a workbook's structure, what kinds of changes are affected?

5 What is a digital signature?

6 What is IRM?

7 When should you use the Document Inspector?

Unit 9

Templates and settings

Unit time: 35 minutes

Complete this unit, and you'll know how to:

A Change Excel's default application settings.

B Use Excel's built-in templates to create invoices.

C Create and manage custom templates.

Topic A: Application settings

Explanation

The Excel Options dialog box contains settings for specifying how Excel starts and operates. Often, though, the default settings don't provide you with the environment that's best for your working habits. For example, you might want to change the format in which data appears, or change the number of worksheets in a new workbook. You might want to personalize your copy of Excel or save your worksheets in a different location. The Excel Options dialog box, shown in Exhibit 7-6, can be used to modify these and other settings.

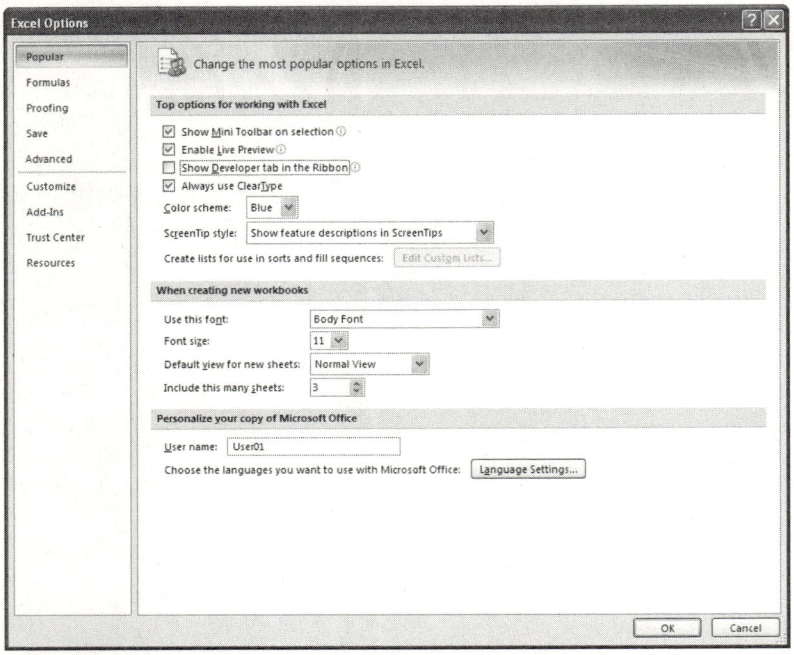

Exhibit 9-1: The Excel Options dialog box

The Excel Options dialog box

To open the Excel Options dialog box, click the Office Button and click Excel Options. The Excel Options dialog box contains the following pages:

Page	Description
Popular	Basic options for setting application defaults.
Formulas	Options that set defaults for how formulas are calculated in a worksheet.
Proofing	Options to configure the spelling checker and other correction features.
Save	Options related to saving workbook files.
Advanced	Advanced options for setting application defaults, including editing and display options.
Customize	Options for adding frequently used commands to the Quick Access toolbar, as well as commands that do not occur on one of the standard tabs.
Add-ins	Options for managing plug-ins and other extensions that can be developed for Excel.
Trust Center	Options related to privacy and computer security.
Resources	Online resources for upgrading and repairing Microsoft Office.

Do it!

A-1: Exploring application settings

Here's how	Here's why
1 Create a new, blank workbook	
2 Click 	The Office Button displays a menu.
Choose **Excel Options**	
3 Select **Popular**	This page includes basic display and personalization options.
Under "Personalize your copy of Microsoft Office," observe the User name box	Your instructor entered a user name for you earlier. You'll change it to your own name.
In the User name box, enter your name	
Under "Top options for working with Excel," click **Edit Custom Lists**	The Custom Lists dialog box appears. You'll create a custom list that can be used in Outlander Spices workbooks.
4 In the List entries box, enter **North, South, East, Central, West**	(Enter the commas, along with the region names.) Many of Outlander Spices' sales worksheets are organized by sales regions. A predefined list of regions would be useful when creating worksheets.
Click **Add**	 The list of sales regions joins the other sequences in the Custom lists box.
Click **OK**	To close the Options dialog box and return to the Excel Options dialog box.

5 Select **Customize**	You can use this page to add frequently used commands to the Quick Access toolbar. You can also add commands that are not on one of the standard Ribbon tabs.
In the Popular Commands list, select **Print Preview**	To select print-related commands.
Click **Add**	To put the Print Preview command on the Quick Access toolbar for all documents.
6 Click **OK**	To close the Excel Options dialog box and apply the changes.

Topic B: Built-in templates

Explanation

You can use a template to create multiple workbooks that have the same settings. A *template* is a workbook with predefined settings on which you can base new workbooks. Templates can contain labels and other data, formatting, styles, and functionality such as formulas.

The Templates dialog box

If you have an Internet connection, you have access to Microsoft Office Online, from which you can download hundreds of templates for business, education, and personal use. You can view these templates by choosing File, New and selecting a template category and subcategory, as shown in Exhibit 9-2.

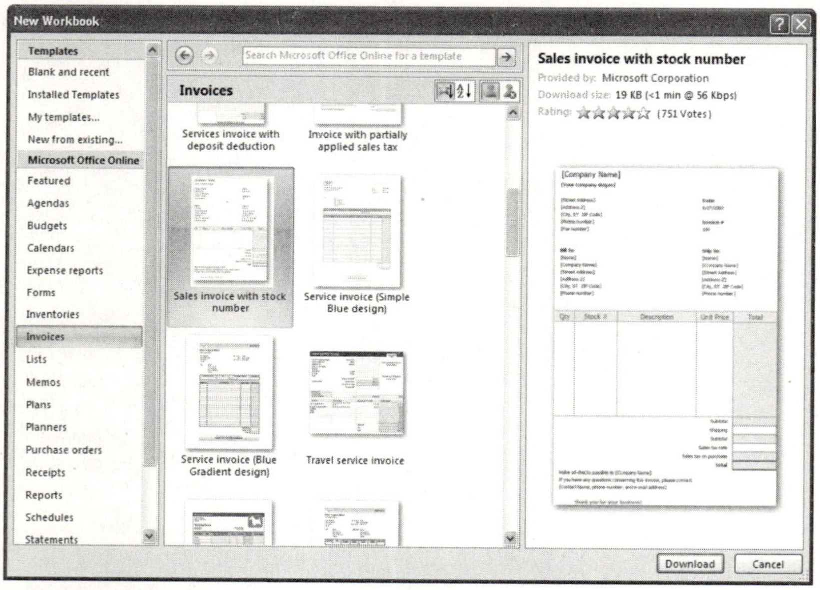

Exhibit 9-2: Invoice templates in the New Workbook dialog box

Creating a workbook from a template

You can use one of the Sales invoice templates to create invoices you send to customers, such as the example shown in Exhibit 9-3. In a sales invoice, you can include company details (such as name and address), customer details, order details, and payment details.

To use the "Sales invoice with stock number" template:

1. Open the New Workbook dialog box.
2. In the templates list, under Microsoft Office Online, click the Invoices category.
3. Find the "Sales invoice with stock number" template.
4. Double-click the template to download and open it. When the Microsoft Office Genuine Advantage dialog box appears, click Continue.

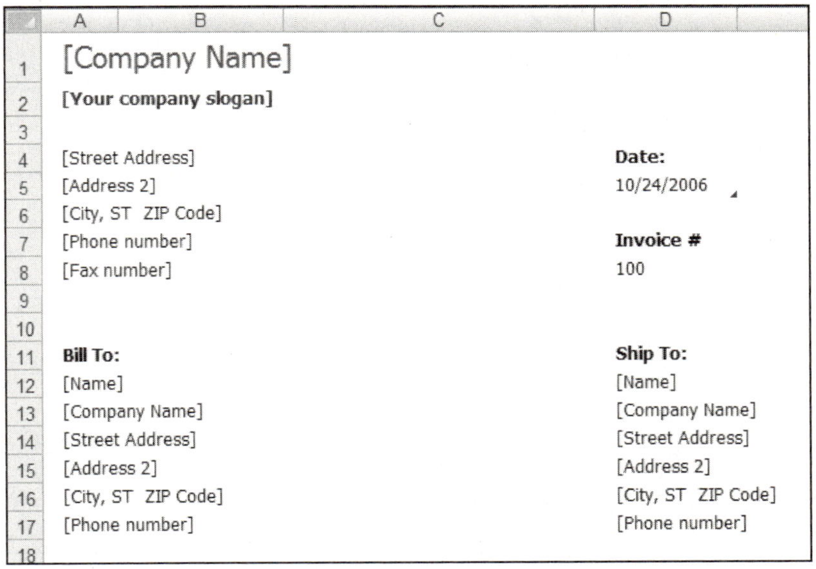

Exhibit 9-3: A portion of the "Sales invoice with stock number" template

Do it!

B-1: Using a downloaded template

Here's how	Here's why
1 Open the New Workbook dialog box	Click the Office Button and choose New.
In the Template list, under Microsoft Office Online, click **Invoices**	To display the templates available in the Invoices category.
2 Observe the template thumbnails	You can see what each template looks like.
Double-click **Sales invoice with stock number**	The Microsoft Office Genuine Advantage message box appears briefly.
Click **Continue**	To download the template. When the template finishes downloading, the title bar of the new workbook displays "Sales invoice with stock number1," indicating that this is a worksheet based on that template.
3 Open the Save As dialog box	
Navigate to the current unit folder	If necessary.
Edit the File name box to read **My OS sales invoice**	
Click **Save**	To save the workbook with the new name.
4 Click **Company Name**	In the upper-left corner of the worksheet.
Enter the company details, as shown	Outlander Spices **adding spice to your life** 61 Rock Creek Drive Attn: Fulfillment Center Portland, OR 97201 555.735.0948 555.735.0950
5 Enter the Bill To details, as shown	**Bill To:** Adam Hayward Spice of Life, Inc. 7 Ulster Street Denver, CO 80237 720.528.1700

6 Enter the indicated Qty, Description, and Unit Price details

Qty	Stock #	Description	Unit Price	Total
25	1701	Cassia	$750.00	**$18,750.00**
45	1719	Cilantro Flakes	$800.00	**$36,000.00**

The Total value for each product is calculated automatically when you enter the Qty and Unit Price. The Subtotal and Total values for the entire invoice are also calculated automatically.

7 Select A37

Observe the formula bar

This cell refers to the company name you entered.

8 Edit A39 to read as shown

Kim Leong, 555.735.0955, kleong@outlanderspices.com

9 Update and close the workbook

Topic C: Creating and managing templates

This topic covers the following Microsoft Certified Application Specialist exam objective for Excel 2007.

#	Objective
5.4.2	**Using the correct format, save a workbook as a template, a Web page, a macro-enabled document, or another appropriate document.** • Save as a template

Custom templates

Explanation

If the templates provided in Excel do not contain all the functionality you need, you can create your own templates—either from scratch or by modifying one of the Microsoft templates. You can use custom templates to create and maintain multiple workbooks with the same formatting, styles, content, and functionality.

To create a template:

1. Open or create the workbook on which you want to base the template.
2. Open the Save As dialog box.
3. From the Save as type list, select Excel Template.
4. In the File name box, enter a name for the template.
5. Click Save.

Do it!

C-1: Creating a template

Here's how	Here's why
1 Open Sample test	(From the current unit folder.) You'll use this workbook as the basis for a new template. The Sample test workbook contains two linked worksheets: Observations and Results.
2 Open the Save As dialog box	
From the Save as type list, select **Excel Template**	To create a template file based on this workbook. The Save in box contains "Templates," indicating that Excel saves templates in the Templates folder by default. The File name box contains "Sample test," indicating that Excel saves the template with the name of the workbook on which it's based.
Click **Save**	To create the Sample test template.
3 Close the template	
4 Open the New Workbook dialog box	You'll create a workbook based on the Sample test template.
In the Templates list, select **My templates...**	To open the New dialog box.
Select **Sample test**	
Click **OK**	The workbook opens in read-only format.
5 Save the file as an Excel Workbook with the file name **My test**	In the current unit folder.
6 Under Sample Details, enter the indicated information	**Product**: Anise Seed; **Sample Code**: S001; **Test Type**: T005; **Sample Date**: 6/16/2006
7 Activate the Results sheet	Formulas in the Results worksheet automatically carry over data from the Observations worksheet.
8 Update and close the workbook	

Table for step 6:

Product	Anise Seed
Sample Code	S001
Test Type	T005
Sample Date	6/16/2006

Modifying templates

Explanation

You might sometimes need to modify custom templates. To do so:

1. Display the Open dialog box.
2. Navigate to the template folder, select the template to be modified, and click Open.
3. Make your changes and update the template.

Do it!

C-2: Modifying a template

Here's how	Here's why
1 Open the Sample test template	It's stored in the Templates folder. For a typical Excel installation in Windows XP, the folder will be C:\Documents and Settings*User_name*\Application Data\Microsoft\Templates.
2 In A11, enter **Tested By**	
3 Copy the contents of A11	
Activate the Results sheet	
Paste the contents in A11	
4 Activate the Observations sheet	To ensure that this is the active worksheet when the template is saved.
5 Update and close the template	
6 Create a workbook based on the Sample test template	You can see the changes you made in the template.
7 Close the workbook	You need not save changes.

Using an alternate template location

Explanation

When you save a workbook as a template in Windows XP, by default the template is saved in the C:\Documents and Settings*User_name*\Application Data\Microsoft\Templates folder. If you have a template stored in a location other than this default folder, it will not automatically appear in the New Workbook dialog box.

To specify an alternate template location and have Excel open those templates automatically:

1. Open the Excel Options dialog box.
2. In the category list, choose Advanced.
3. Under General, in the "At startup, open all files in" box, type the path to the folder containing the template files.
4. Click OK.

Do it!

C-3: Specifying an alternate template location

Here's how	Here's why
1 Open the Excel Options dialog box	
In the category list, select **Advanced**	
Under General, in the "At startup, open all files" box, enter the path for the Alternate Template folder	Depending on your installation, this might be C:\Student Data\Unit_09\Alternate Template.
Click **OK**	To close the Excel Options dialog box.
2 Close any open workbooks and close Excel	The new option won't take effect until you restart Excel.
Restart Excel	
Close the blank workbook	
3 Open the New Workbook dialog box	
4 Select **My templates...**	The New dialog box opens with the Alt template in the Alternate Template folder selected.
5 Click **Cancel**	To close the New dialog box and return to the New Workbook dialog box.
Click **Cancel**	To close the New Workbook dialog box.
6 Open the Excel Options dialog box	
Select **Advanced**	If necessary.
Delete the path for alternate templates	Under General, in the "At startup, open all files in" box.
Click **OK**	The alternate template location is removed.

Unit summary: Templates and settings

Topic A In this topic, you learned about Excel's **application settings**. You learned how to change defaults that control the way Excel operates and displays data.

Topic B In this topic, you learned about **templates**, which can be used as a basis to create multiple workbooks. You also learned how to download and use a template from Microsoft Office Online.

Topic C In this topic, you learned how to **create custom templates** that contain your preferred formatting, styles, content, and functionality. You also learned how to modify a custom template and specify an alternate location for template files.

Independent practice activity

In this activity, you'll add a command to the Quick Access toolbar. You'll also download and save a template. Then, you'll use the template to create an invoice for a customer.

1 Add the Open (FileOpen) command to the Quick Access toolbar.

2 Create a workbook based on the "Sales invoice with stock number" template (re-downloaded from Microsoft Office Online), and save the workbook as **My spice house invoice** in the current unit folder.

3 Customize the form to include company details, such as name and address.

4 Save the workbook as a template named **My OS invoice**.

5 Close the template.

6 Create a workbook based on the My OS invoice template, and save it with the default file name.

7 In the My OS invoice1 worksheet, enter customer details as shown in Exhibit 9-4.

8 Update and close the workbook.

9 Close Excel.

Bill To:
The Spice House
Attn: Dave Skippington
411 Princeton Ave

Astoria, OR 87103
555.563.2440

Ship To:
The Spice House
Attn: Dave Skippington
411 Princeton Ave

Astoria, OR 87103
555.563.2440

Qty	Stock #	Description	Unit Price	Total
20	1735	Cinnamon	$650.00	**$13,000.00**
15	1761	Nutmeg	$300.00	**$4,500.00**
25	1745	Bay Leaf	$400.00	**$10,000.00**

Exhibit 9-4: The customer details for Step 7

Review questions

1 What worksheet elements can be contained in a template?

2 Where can you view Excel's built-in templates?

3 List the steps you would use to modify a custom template.

4 When you save a workbook as a template on a Windows XP computer, in what folder is it saved by default?

5 If a template is stored in a location other than the default folder, it will not automatically appear in the New Workbook dialog box. True or false?

Course summary

This summary contains information to help you bring the course to a successful conclusion. Using this information, you will be able to:

A Use the summary text to reinforce what you've learned in class.

B Determine the next courses in this series (if any), as well as any other resources that might help you continue to learn about Excel 2007.

Topic A: Course summary

Use the following summary text to reinforce what you've learned in class.

Unit summaries

Unit 1

In this unit, you learned how to switch between workbooks and copy a worksheet to another workbook. Then, you learned how to create **3-D formulas** to perform calculations based on data from multiple worksheets, and how to add a **Watch window** to a cell. Then, you created **links** to data in a different workbook, and you saw that Excel automatically updates data in the destination workbook when you change the data in the source workbook. You learned how to **redirect links**. Finally, you learned how to save an arrangement of open workbooks as a **workspace**.

Unit 2

In this unit, you learned how to apply **special number formats** to ZIP codes, Social Security numbers, and phone numbers, and you learned how to control the display of zero values. Then, you created **custom number formats**. Next, you learned how to use formulas to format text. You observed Excel's built-in **styles** and **themes**, and you learned how to create, modify, and apply styles and themes. You learned how to **merge cells**, change the orientation of text in cells, and split merged cells. Finally, you learned how to add color and a watermark to a worksheet background.

Unit 3

In this unit, you learned how to create an **outline** to summarize data by levels, and you learned how to use the **Consolidate command** to summarize data from several ranges. Finally, you learned how to create automatic **subtotals** to divide a list with summary information.

Unit 4

In this unit, you learned how to create and edit **named ranges** to make formulas easier to understand. You used these names in formulas, and created names automatically from row and column headings. Finally, you created **3-D names** that span multiple sheets.

Unit 5

In this unit, you learned that a **list** is made up of field names, fields, and records. You learned how to **sort** a list by the information in one or more of its columns. You also learned how to use the **AutoFilter** command to display only rows that meet certain criteria. Next, you learned how to use the **Custom AutoFilter** dialog box to specify multiple conditions, using comparison criteria and comparison operators. Then, you created a **criteria range** to specify complex search conditions based on multiple column headings, and you learned how to **copy filtered data** to a new location. You then learned how to create **tables** and how to automatically add rows and columns. You applied **structured referencing** to use column names in formulas. Finally, you renamed tables and used table and column names in formulas outside the table.

Unit 6

In this unit, you learned how to save a worksheet as a **Web page**. You learned how to use the Web Page Preview command to see how a worksheet will look before it is saved as a Web page. Then, you **published** a worksheet as a Web page and used the AutoRepublish feature. Next, you learned how to insert **hyperlinks** in a workbook, and learned that clicking a hyperlink opens a Web page in a browser. Finally, you learned how to publish a workbook as a **PDF file** and how to send a workbook via **e-mail**.

Unit 7

In this unit, you learned how to adjust the **scale** of a chart. You learned how to format **data points** and explode slices in a pie chart to highlight data. Then, you learned how to create a **combination chart** by using two value axes. You also learned how to add a **trendline** to a chart. Then, you learned how to add, format, and move **graphic elements** in a chart. Finally, you learned how to insert a **picture** in a worksheet.

Unit 8

In this unit, you learned how to trace **precedent** and **dependent cells** and how to **trace errors** by using the Formula Auditing tools. Next, you learned how to use **comments** to add information to worksheets and workbooks. Then, you learned how to **protect** a worksheet to prevent unauthorized users from making changes, and you learned how to **unlock cells** that users should be allowed to modify. Next, you learned about **Information Rights Management** and **digital signatures**. Then, you learned how to **share workbooks** and merge copies of shared workbooks. You learned how to **track changes** in a workbook and accept or reject tracked changes. Finally, you learned how to use the **Document Inspector** and how to mark workbooks as final.

Unit 9

In this unit, you learned about Excel's **application settings**, and learned how to change settings that control the way Excel operates and displays data. Next, you learned about using **templates** to create documents such as sales invoices. Then, you learned how to create and modify templates containing any formatting, styles, content, and functionality you want. Finally, you learned how to specify an **alternate location** for template files.

Topic B: Continued learning after class

It is impossible to learn to use any software effectively in a single day. To get the most out of this class, you should begin working with Excel 2007 to perform real tasks as soon as possible. Course Technology also offers resources for continued learning.

Next courses in this series

This is the second course in this series. The next courses in this series are:

- *Excel 2007: Advanced*
- *Excel 2007: Power User*
- *Excel 2007: VBA Programming*

Other resources

For more information, visit www.course.com.

Excel 2007: Intermediate

Quick reference

Button	Shortcut keys	Function
		Displays the Borders menu.
		Opens a dialog box for the current Ribbon group.
		Merges the cells in a column or row and centers the text.
		Displays the Orientation menu, which controls the direction in which text runs.
		Centers text vertically in a cell.
	CTRL + B	Makes text bold.
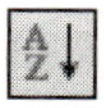		Sorts a list in ascending order.
		Clears a filter applied to the selected range.
		Collapses a dialog box.
		Expands a dialog box.
		Displays the Fill Color gallery.
	C + T	Inserts a table.
	S + F2	Inserts a new comment into a cell.
		Displays error-checking options.

Button	Shortcut keys	Function
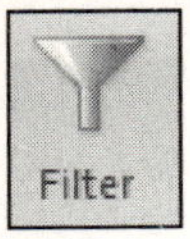	C + SHIFT + L	Turns filtering on or off.
		Protects a worksheet by preventing unwanted changes in the data.
		Protects a workbook by preventing unwanted changes in its structure.
		Shares the workbook so that multiple users can access and/or change the data.
		Changes the selected chart to a different type.

Glossary

3-D Formula
A formula that refers to the same cell or range in multiple worksheets.

Calculation
The process of computing and displaying the results of formulas.

Cell Orientation
Refers to the direction of text flow in a cell.

Combination Chart
Includes two or more graph types in a single chart.

Conditional Formatting
Formatting that is applied to data only if a specific criteria is satisfied.

Criteria Range
A group of cells that contain a set of search conditions.

Dependent Cell
Relies on the value of another cell.

Destination Workbook
A workbook that contains a formula with an external reference.

Digital Certificate
An attachment that guarantees security for a file.

Digital Signature
An electronic security stamp that is used to authenticate files that are sent through the Internet.

Docked
A toolbar state used to describe when a toolbar is attached to an edge of the program window.

External Link
That part of a formula in one workbook that refers to a cell, range, or name in another workbook. Also called an external reference.

External Reference
That part of a formula in one workbook that refers to a cell, range, or name in another workbook. Also called an external link.

Field
A column of data in a list.

Field Name
A column heading, which appears in the first row of a list.

Floating
A toolbar state used to describe when a toolbar appears to hover over the worksheet.

Freeze Panes
A command that locks row or column headings in place so that when you scroll, these headings will remain visible.

Leader Line
Used in a chart to connect a data label to its associated data point.

List
A series of rows containing related data.

Outline
Organizes worksheet by grouping it in levels of detail.

Precedent Cell
Provides data to a specific cell.

Print Title
Text that you want to print as a heading on all pages.

Record
A row of data in a list.

Short Menu
A menu that doesn't display all available commands when you first open it.

Sizing Handles
Appear as small squares or circles around the border of a selected picture and are used to change its height and width.

Smart Menu
A menu that displays the commands that you use most frequently.

Sorting
Organizing the data in a list in ascending or descending order by the contents of one or more columns in the list.

Source Workbook
The workbook to which an external reference refers.

Splitting
Dividing a worksheet into panes so that you can see different areas simultaneously.

Style
A collection of formats that are saved and applied as a group.

Template
A workbook with predefined settings on which you can base new workbooks.

Trendline
A graphical representation of drifts or variations in a data series.

Watch Window
A dialog box that displays values and formulas in another linked worksheet without navigating there.

Workspace
A logical container of related workbooks that retains page setups, window sizes, and display settings.

Index

M

N

O

P

Q

R

S

T

U

W

www.AXZOPress.com